T0077906

Other Books by the Author

From the Pew to the Pulpit	Published: 08/29/2007
Isaiah 26:3-4 "Perfect Peace"	Published: 09/16/2010*
Isaiah 26:3-4 "Perfect Peace" The Last Single Digit	Published: 02/15/2012*
Isaiah 26:3-4 "Perfect Peace III" Silver and Gold	Published: 10/29/2012*
Isaiah 26:3-4 "Perfect Peace IV" The Kingdom Number	Published: 04/15/2013*
Isaiah 26:3-4 "Perfect Peace V" 2541	Published: 09/13/2013*
Isaiah 26:3-4 "Perfect Peace VI" Zacchaeus	Published: 02/28/2014
Isaiah 26:3-4 "Perfect Peace VII" Eleven	Published: 10/30/2014*
Isaiah 26:3-4 "Perfect Peace VIII" Prayer	Published: 05/21/2015*
Isaiah 26:3-4 "Perfect Peace IX" Sixteen	Published: 10/24/2015*
Isaiah 26:3-4 "Perfect Peace X" Dreams	Published: 04/12/2016
Isaiah 26:3-4 "Perfect Peace XI" Door	Published: 02/13/2017
Isaiah 26:3-4 "Perfect Peace XII" River	Published: 08/02/2017
Isaiah 26:3-4 "Perfect Peace XIII" 1 Kings 19:1-18	Published: 12/18/2017
Isaiah 26:3-4 "Perfect Peace XIV" G – Men	Published: 05/03/2018*
Isaiah 26:3-4 "Perfect Peace XV" 11:29	Published: 07/26/2018
Isaiah 26:3-4 "Perfect Peace XVI" Shoes	Published: 10/31/2018*
Isaiah 26:3-4 "Perfect Peace XVII" Arrow	Published: 01/25/2019*
Isaiah 26:3-4 "Perfect Peace XVIII" Midnight	Published: 04/26/2019
Isaiah 26:3-4 "Perfect Peace XIX" Eyes	Published: 08/20/2019
Isaiah 26:3-4 "Perfect Peace XX" Judges 4:1-16	Published: 12/18/2019
Isaiah 26:3-4 "Perfect Peace XXI" Winter	Published: 03/22/2020

PS: On 5/25/2019, I noticed that some of the book published dates vary slightly from AuthorHouse, depending on which bookstore site you visit. They have been modified to reflect AuthorHouse's publication date, indicated by an *.

ISAIAH 26:3-4

"PERFECT PEACE XXII"

Flowering Plants

VANESSA RAYNER

authorHOUSE®

AuthorHouse™
1663 Liberty Drive
Bloomington, IN 47403
www.authorhouse.com
Phone: 833-262-8899

Published by AuthorHouse 09/03/2020

ISBN: 978-1-7283-7262-4 (sc)
ISBN: 978-1-7283-7261-7 (e)

Library of Congress Control Number: 2020916793

Print information available on the last page.

This book is printed on acid-free paper.

The Scriptures' quotations are taken from the KJV, NIV, NLT, and WEB.

The King James Version present on the Bible Gateway matches the 1987 printing. The KJV is public domain in the United States.

The Holy Bible, New International Version, NIV Copyright© 1973, 1978, 1984, 2011 by Biblia, Inc. Used by permission. All rights reserved worldwide.

Holy Bible, New Living Translation copyright© 1996, 2004, 2007 by Tyndale House Foundation. Used by permission of Tyndale House Publishers Inc., Carol Stream, Illinois 60188. All rights reserved.

World English Bible present on the Bible Gateway is a public domain. It is an updated revision of the American Standard Version of the Holy Bible first published in 1901.

CONTENTS

A GIFT . . .

*P*resented to

_____

*F*rom

_____

*D*ate

_____

Jesus, the Rose of Sharon and the Lily of the Valleys
Song of Solomon 2:1

THEME

The message of **Isaiah 26:3 – 4** is "Perfect Peace." This message is the distinct and unifying composition of this book with the subtitle Flowering Plants.

A Song of Praise

Thou wilt keep him in perfect peace, whose mind is stayed on thee: because he trusted in thee. Trust ye in the LORD for ever: for in the LORD Jehovah is everlasting strength.

Isaiah 26:3 – 4 KJV

PRAYER

Thank You Lord, Thank You Lord, Thank You Lord
Hallelujah!
I thank you for another day and another
opportunity to write another book for You.
Oh, Father God, you have been good to me,
and I Thank You for all your many blessings.

I thank You for blessing my family.
And I pray that your people and their
families are being bless,
inspite of the coronavirus pandemic.
Oh Father, I will be the first to admit, I don't
understand everything You do but,
I trust You in everything.
Father, I pray that your people will remember,
there is nothing too hard for You,
And You promise You will not put
more on us than we can bear.
Father help us to remember to look to the
hills from whence comes our strength.
Our strength comes from You, who
made heaven and earth.

I pray that your people are prospering daily in their
spirit, soul, and body by reading, Perfect Peace Books.
I ask in Jesus' name that the Holy Spirit will
help readers to remember Your word.
I pray the word of God will give them
peace in all life situations.

LORD, I thank you for blessing those
that help Your work go forth.
Your word made it clear that You will
reward those that bless your servant.
It could be through prayer, words of encouragement,
to giving that person a cup of water.

Father, I give you all the Glory, Honor,
and Praise in Jesus' name.

Amen.

AUTHOR'S NOTES

Author notes generally provide a way to add extra information to one's book that may be awkward and inappropriate to include in the text of the book itself. It offers supplemental contextual details on the aspects of the book. It can help readers understand the book content and the background details of the book better. The times and dates of researching, reading, and gathering this information are not included; mostly when I typed on it.

1943; Saturday, 21 March 2020; At this time, I'm not sure what the title of this book is going to be or what Father God wants me to write about, but I'm ready. Yesterday, the final changes were made in the book titled <u>Isaiah 26:3 – 4 "Perfect Peace XXI" Winter</u>. I was sitting in my living room, praying about the coronavirus pandemic. I'm about to watch the last 10 minutes of "Planet Earth: Blue Planet II" on channel 264 BBCA, and probably the next program titled "Seasonal Wonderlands." The amazing planet and creation of Father God. Hallelujah!

0715; Sunday, 22 March 2020; After watching channel 264 BBCA last night, I was astonished to learn that Svalbard has 6 straight months of endless freezing nights with temperature ranging from 8.6 to -4.0 Fahrenheit. The 6 months of endless daylight occurs in late March, and last to late September; the temperature ranges from 37.4 to 44.6 Fahrenheit. What took my breath away was how the flowers immerse from under the thick frozen ice-covered land to bloom during the months of daylight. God Is Truly Amazing . . . Praise God!

1826; Monday, 23 March 2020

1707; Tuesday, 24 March 2020

1701; Wednesday, 25 March 2020; Happy B'day to me.

1701; Thursday, 26 March 2020

1659; Friday, 27 March 2020

0405; Saturday, 28 March 2020

0551; Sunday, 29 March 2020

1733; Monday, 30 March 2020

1718; Friday, 01 April 2020

0609; Sunday, 05 April 2020

0717; Monday, 06 April 2020; Today is my oldest sister's Birthday, Easter. I woke up with muscle spasm. The Coronavirus issues and limited activities are trying to take its hold on me. I'm binding it in the Name of Jesus. I haven't had muscle spasms like this in over 4 or 5 years. I am staying home today. Thank You, Jesus, I Blessed Your Holy Name! Oh Yea, . . . Last night at 9:30 pm CST, I attended Bro. Miller's Hour of Prayer Teleconference. We all had a glorious time in the LORD! He asked me to give the closing prayer. I let Father God have his way, and I prayed and prayed and prayed. My, my, my, my . . . . Hallelujah! The LORD is great and worthy to be praised.

1715; Tuesday, 07 April 2020

1704; Wednesday, 08 April 20

1701; Thursday, 09 April 2020

0647; Friday, 10 April 2020; Good Friday

0552; Saturday, 11 April 2020

0808; Sunday, 12 April 2020; Happy Easter

1734; Monday, 13 April 2020

2021; Wednesday, 15 April 2020

1705; Thursday, 16 April 2020
2213; Friday, 17 April 2020
0000; Saturday, 18 April 2020
0802; Sunday, 19 April 2020
1716; Monday, 20 April 2020
1752; Tuesday, April 21, 2020
1726; Wednesday, 22 April 2020
1931; Friday, 24 April 2020
1749; Sunday, 26 April 2020
1659; Tuesday, 28 April 2020
0729; Saturday, 02 May 2020
0000; Sunday, 03 May 2020
1914; Monday, 04 May 2020
0448; Thursday, 07 May 2020
0414; Friday, 08 May 2020
0613; Sunday, 10 May 2020; Mother's Day
1840; Monday, 11 May 2020
1711; Tuesday, 12 May 2020
1947; Wednesday, 13 May 2020
1945; Friday, 15 May 2020
0631; Saturday, 16 May 2020
0540; Sunday, 17 May 2020
1900; Monday, 18 May 2020
1737; Wednesday, 20 May 2020
1817; Thursday, 21 May 2020
0757; Saturday, 23 May 2020
0512; Sunday, 24 May 2020
0607; Monday, 25 May 2020; Memorial Day
0629; Wednesday, 27 May 2020

1657; Thursday, 28 May 2020

0540; Saturday, 30 May 2020

0604; Sunday, 31 May 2020

1634; Monday, 01 June 2020

1706; Tuesday, 02 June 2020

0647; Wednesday, 03 June 2020; Eye Specialist Appointment today. I am praying and singing all is well. Hallelujah!

1714; Thursday, 04 June 2020; All was well. Hallelujah!

1738; Friday, 05 June 2020

0703; Saturday, 06 June 2020

0000; Sunday, 07 June 2020

1658; Monday, 08 June 2020

2032; Wednesday, 10 June 2020

0652; Thursday, 11 June 2020

1734; Friday, 12 June 2020

0603; Saturday, 13 June 2020

0530; Sunday, 14 June 2020; Happy Birthday to my brother, AD

0344; Monday, 15 June 2020; Praise God! I will be home for 2 days for Conway Plumbing Services to work on my front bathroom plumbing grouping. Conway Services came out Saturday; I thought I needed a wax ring because the toilet was leaking at the bottom on the floor. Mr. Joseph had me flushed the toilet, run water in the bathtub, and when we looked under the crawl space of the house, water was profusely leaking from the tub, toilet, and sink piping. The piping is cast-iron, so all that will be replaced, and tied into the previous underground sewer line, which was replaced about 2 decades ago. The cost is $6,900, and I Thank God, I have a house that I can repair; I give God Praise because it could have been worse, and I Worship God in spite of because He deserves all the Glory, Honor, and Praise. . . . . Shatata . . . . . I'm going to work on Father's book before Conway Services arrive this morning. Hallelujah!

0614; Tuesday, 16 June 2020

0247; Wednesday, 17 June 2020

1804; Thursday, 18 June 2020

1658; Friday, 19 June 2020

0605; Saturday, 20 June 2020

0242; Sunday, 21 June 2020; Happy Father Day!

1828; Monday, 22 June 2020

1746; Wednesday, 24 June 2020

1704; Thursday, 25 June 2020

0600; Saturday, June 27, 2020

0119; Sunday, 28 June 2020

1658; Monday, 29 June 2020

1838; Tuesday, 30 June 2020

1718; Wednesday, 01 July 2020

1744; Thursday, 02 July 2020

0743; Friday, 03 July 2020

0750; Saturday, 04 July 2020; 4th of July

0536; Sunday, 05 July 2020

1805; Monday, 06 July 2020

1728; Tuesday, 07 July 2020

1711; Wednesday, 08 July 2020

1656; Thursday, 09 July 2020; Happy Birthday to Alvin L. Jackson

1915; Friday, 10 July 2020

0656; Saturday, 11 July 2020

0444; Sunday, 12 July 2020

1746; Monday, 13 July 2020

1819; Tuesday, 14 July 2020

1705; Wednesday, 15 July 2020

1703; Thursday, 16 July 2020

1729; Friday, 17 July 2020

0442; Saturday, 18 July 2020

0418; Sunday, 19 July 2020; Happy Birthday Mom "Ulyer Moore"

1700; Monday, 20 July 2020

2010; Tuesday, 21 July 2020

1933; Wednesday, 22 July 2020

1701; Thursday, 23 July 2020

1850; Friday, 24 July 2020

0144; Saturday, 25 July 2020

0633; Sunday, 26 July 2020; Happy Birthday to my youngest Sister, Regina

1707; Monday, 27 July 2020

1734; Thursday, 30 July 2020

0655; Friday, 31 July 2020; Will be proofreading, until I go to the doctor's office.

0534; Saturday, 01 August 2020

0208; Sunday, 02 August 2020

1753; Monday, 03 August 2020

1732; Tuesday, 04 August 2020

1700; Wednesday, 05 August 2020

1940; Thursday, 06 August 2020

0624; Friday, 07 August 2020; I woke up this morning, and once I finished praying, the unction of the Holy Spirit instructed me to list the flowering plants discussed in this book. I just sent this manuscript to my phone e-mail to start looking through the manuscript on my hour lunch break. Isn't He so, so, so wonderful? Praise God.

0556; Saturday, 08 August 2020

0105; Sunday, 09 August 2020

1755; Monday, 10 August 2020

1803; Thursday, 13 August 2020; I'm about to send manuscript to AuthorHouse.

PREFACE

Isaiah 26:3-4, "Perfect Peace XXII" Flowering Plants

The book <u>Isaiah 26:3-4, "Perfect Peace XXII" Flowering Plants</u>, is the 22nd book in a series called Isaiah 26:3-4, "Perfect Peace." Praise God.

It all started from how I drew near to the LORD in my workplace by keeping my mind on Him. I related numbers you see throughout the day, everywhere, on almost everything on Him, His word, biblical events, and facts to give me peace in the midst of chaos.

It's our desire for you to discover the power of the Holy Spirit by numbers, words, places, people, and things surrounding the word Flowers.

Remember, the LORD Jesus <u>PROMISED us TRIBULATION</u> while we were in this world.

These things, I have spoken unto you,
that in me ye might have peace.
In the world ye shall have tribulation:
But be of good cheer; I have overcome the world.
John 16:33 KJV

However, we have been <u>PROMISED His PEACE</u> while we endure these trials, tribulations, troubles, and tests. Perfect Peace is given only to those whose mind and heart reclines upon the LORD. God's peace is increased in us according to the knowledge of His Holy Word.

Grace and peace be multiplied unto you
through the knowledge of God,
and of Jesus our LORD.
2 Peter 1:2 KJV

THANKS . . .

As a disciple of the LORD Jesus Christ, I have learned true success comes when we are seeking and striving to do God's purpose for our lives. Our real happiness lies in doing God's will, even in the midst of our trials, tests, temptations, and tribulations, but not in fame and fortune.

I appreciate your support. Thanks for helping me spread the "Perfect Peace Series" through your e-mail, Facebook, Twitter, LinkedIn, Instagram, Tumblr, Messenger, or other accounts to your family, friends, neighbors, co-workers, church family, internet social friends, and associates.

Remember, you may not know until you get to heaven just how much a song you sung, kind words spoken by you, a book you suggested reading, or gave as a gift, at the right moment, encourage that person to keep on going when a few minutes before they were tempted to give up on life and their walk with the LORD.

Your lovingkindness to this ministry is greatly appreciated.

ACKNOWLEDGEMENTS

I wish to express my sincere gratitude to "Our Heavenly Father" for his guidance, patience, and lovingkindness throughout the writing of this book.

~~~

INTRODUCTION

For Those Who Want to Be Kept In "Perfect Peace"

<u>Isaiah 26:3 – 4, "Perfect Peace XXII" Flowering Plants</u> was prepared and written to open your mind to a "Perfect Peace" that comes only from God. I'm striving through this book to elevate you into a "Unique and Profound" awareness of God's presence around you at all times.

According to some people, it's hard to keep your mind on the LORD. While most Christians will agree that if you keep your mind stayed on the LORD, He will keep you in "Perfect Peace." Therefore, so many people enjoy going to church on Sundays and attending midweek services for the peace and joy that they receive, but only for a short time.

You can experience the peace of the LORD throughout the day and every day. His unspeakable joy, his strength, his "Perfect Peace" during the storm, whether it's at work, home, college, school, etc. You can also experience this peace, even when your day is going well.

This concept of this book was placed in my spirit by our Father, which art in heaven, to help me when he allowed Satan to test me at my workplace until he finished molding me into a MAP; (Minister/Ambassador/Pastor).

Throughout these pages, I will be focussing on biblical events and facts surrounding Flowering Plants. However, I am sure much more can be said concerning Flowering Plants, so these chapter subjects serve merely as an introduction and are not exhaustive by any means.

DEDICATION

This book is dedicated to the Anthophiles, Naturalists, Botanists, Plant Nurseries, and all the individuals who love to plant and grow flowers, then nurture, cherish, and watch them blossom.

I also like to dedicate this book to my mom, Ulyer Moore (July 19, 1925 – September 6, 1983), who loved and grew roses, especially the multi-colored. She also grew other plants in our backyard, like collard greens, turnips, tomatoes, okra, cucumbers, butter beans, green peas, wild green onions, and sweet potatoes, and a few small round watermelons just for me. Smile . . .

I would also like to dedicate this book to my mother's mom, who is my grandmother, Virgie Lee Mobley (June 14, 1905 – August 15, 1999), who lived in Starkville, Mississippi. She had a large beautiful flower garden that started from the dirt road to her front porch, approximately the size of half a basketball court (47 x 25 feet). In between the flower garden was a narrow dirt path that led to the long wooden front porch that set up high. If you stretched out both of your hands, you could touch the flowers on both sides of the path.

I clearly remember the tall sunflower plants the most, which were taller than me. I can remember smelling the sweet honey suckler in the air while we played on the porch. I can still visualize the variety of colorful growing plants with the butterflies, bumblebees, and hummingbirds going from flower to flower. If you are facing the front of the house, on the far left was orchard trees of bright green apples.

CHAPTER 1
FLOWERS

A flower or flowers is a special part of a plant. The flower is considered the reproductive organs of a flowering plant. A flower is also known as a bloom or blossom of a plant. Bloom refers to the flower at its full development, and blossom describes a flower that is in the early stages of developing into the full bloom.

The flower is usually the most colorful part of most plants, and some plants form fruit. The flower(s) comes first, which requires pollination before the fruit can form, and inside most fruits are the seeds that create the next generation of plants. Only some flowers become fruits, a seed-bearing product that develops from the ovary of a flowering plant. Some flowers are edible, some are used as herbs, while others are made into medicine, and even some flowers are poisonous.

A flower can grow separately on the plant or grow as a cluster of flowers arranged on a plant stem. Some species of plants need to be sown every year, and others come back on their own at the right season. The flowering plants can appear in the spring or fall season and then disappear for the remainder of the year. When the plant grows, the flower of the plant will eventually fade, wilt, and die.

A person who studies plants is known as a botanist. The scientific study of plants is known as botany. The plant kingdom includes everything from algae, ferns, flowers, fruits, herb, grasses, legumes, moss, shrubs, trees, vegetables, and vines. The plant kingdom has many different species of plants that live on land and water. According to the Botanists, there are around 320,000 species of plants. These plant species are classified in different divisions, place in scientific groups, and then divided into subgroups.

The flowering plants are the most diverse group of plants, with 64 orders, 416 families, approximately 13,000 known genera and around 290,000 known species.

There are two major groups of flowering plants, the Dicots and Monocots. The dicots flowering plants have two embryonic seed leaves, and there are about 175,000 known species. The most common dicots are shrubs, trees, and broad-leafed flowering plants such as magnolias and roses.

Monocots are the other group of flowering plants, they have one embryonic seed leave, and there are about 60,000 species in this group. The Monocot group includes flowering plants, such as grasses, lilies, and palm trees. The plant embryo is also called the seed embryo, which is part of the seed that contains the earliest development of a plant's roots, stem, and leaves. The seed embryo develops after it is fertilized.

The first leaves produced by the plant are called the cotyledons. They are considered the seed leaves because they are part of the seed embryo of the plant. The cotyledons provide nutrients to the seedling until its leaves develop, spread, and stretch out to begin the process of photosynthesis. Photosynthesis is the process in which plants use sunlight to produce their food. In short, the Monocots emerge with a single nurturing seed leaf, whereas dicots emerge with two nurturing seed leaves.

The 4 essential parts of a flower are called sepals, petals, carpels, and stamen. The sepal is the flower bud covering, which spread open to form the base of the blossom. The petals open and help attract pollinators like bees, insects, and butterflies. The stamen is the flower's male reproductive organ, and it produces the pollen necessary for fertilization, and the carpel is the female reproductive organ of a flower, and once fertilized, it will produce the fruit and seeds. Both the carpel and stamens are surrounded by the petals of the flower, with large bright colors.

Note of Interests: Petals are part of a flower; they are not the flower's leaves. Petals are considered modified leaves that surround the reproductive parts of flowers used to attract pollinators. Modified leaves are a variation that develops to help and protect the survival of plants. Some modified leaves change color to attract insects to the plant; some develop into thorns to protect it.

Flowering plants rely on pollination for reproduction, but nonflowering plants rely on dispersion to continue their life cycle. Nonflowering plants do not produce a flower; mosses and ferns are the two major types of plants that do not produce flowers.

There are many varieties and kinds of flowers in different parts of the world. In the Bible, very few species of flowers are mentioned by name. However, Scholars believe that in

Israel, there are approximately 2,500 plants located in this area, and researchers believe that the Bible mentions around 120 different kinds of plants, directly and indirectly, that blossom in its due season.

Note of Interests: Researchers discovered, in Biblical times, plants, flowers, and trees were given local names by the inhabitant of that territory. In other words, the same flower could have more than one name. One area of people called it by one name, and miles away in a different territory, it would be called by another name.

In the Bible, flowers are used as symbolism for beauty, growth, and temporal things. The word "flower" and "flowers" are mentioned 17 times each.

However, the word "flowers" is only mentioned in the Old Testament, and "flower" is mentioned in the Old and New Testament.

The word "flowers" is mentioned 13 times in the Old Testament, and they are listed below.

1. Exodus (4)
2. Leviticus (2)
3. Numbers (1)
4. 1 Kings (6)
5. 2 Chronicles (2)
6. Song of Solomon (2)

The word "flower" is mentioned 17 times in the Bible; 13 times in the Old Testament and 4 times in the New Testament, and they are listed below.

Old Testament

1. Exodus (2)
2. 1 Samuel (1)
3. Job (2)
4. Psalm (1)
5. Isaiah (6)
6. Nahum (1)

New Testament

1. 1 Corinthians (1)
2. James (2)
3. 1 Peter (1)

The Gospel of Jesus Christ is a beautiful reminder of our glorious LORD, and flowers are used in illuminating this beauty.

The fig tree forms its early fruit; the blossoming vines spread their fragrance. Arise, come, my darling; my beautiful one, come with me.

Song of Solomon 2:13 NIV

His cheeks are like beds of spice yielding perfume. His lips are like lilies dripping with myrrh.

Song of Solomon 5:13 NIV

The LORD uses the image of a flower to describe the life cycle of man. The sunlight shines on a flower, the flower receives its proper nutrients, the correct amount of water, and blossom for a season, but one thing will remain true; the flower will eventually die.

How frail is humanity! How short is life, how full of trouble! We blossom like a flower and then wither.

Job 14:1 – 2 KJV

Our days on earth are like grass; like wildflowers, we bloom and die.

Psalm 103:15 NLT

The grass withers and the flowers fade beneath the breath of the LORD. And so it is with people.

Isaiah 40:8 NLT

As the Scriptures say, "People are like grass; their beauty is like a flower in the field. The grass withers and the flower fades. But the word of the LORD remains forever.

1 Peter 1:24 – 25 NLT

The hot sun rises and the grass withers; the little flower droops and falls, and its beauty fades away. In the same way, the rich will fade away with all of their achievements.

James 1:11 NLT

CHAPTER 2
POMEGRANATE

According to Genesis 2:8, "And the LORD God planted a garden eastward in Eden, and there he put the man whom he had formed." KJV

Question: What was the name of the 4 riverheads that watered the Garden of Eden? *Think and smile . . . The answer is in the back of the book*

1. _____
2. _____
3. Hiddekel
4. _____

PS: The river I couldn't remember, I named that one, for you.

Researchers have been able to identify several flowering plants that might have been in the Garden of Eden, by the word of God, the Bible. Other researchers have visited the area, which is believed to be where the Garden of Eden could have been located.

The pomegranate plant is believed to have been one of the flowers in the Garden of Eden. The scientific name for pomegranate is "Punica granatum." The pomegranate is a fruit-bearing shrub that grows between 10 to 15 ft. high. The pomegranate fruit is delicious, filled with juicy red seeds. It usually ripens around September and grows about the size of an orange. Inside the pomegranate are chambered

red pulp containing many seeds, enclosed in a thick, hard, deep reddish skin. The pomegranate is believed to be one of the oldest known edible fruits, first cultivated in the Middle East.

Note of Interests: Remember, the "scientific name" is a name used by scientists written in Latin, developed by Carl Linnaeus, an 18th century botanist. It's a unique name given to a plant, animal, or single-celled life form used across the world by scientists, regardless of the language they speak or write. A plant can have several "common names," depending on the region, but only one "scientific name." The scientific name always consists of two-names; for example, "Punica granatum." The first word of the scientific name identifies the plant's Genus (Punica), the group of species to which it belongs, and the genus name is capitalized. The word "granatum" is the second name of the scientific name, which is an adjective describing the individual species, and it is in lowercase. There are more than one Punica, but only one Punica granatum.

According to Jewish traditions, the pomegranate is a symbol of righteousness, and it's believed that every fruit has 613 seeds, corresponding with the number of commandments recorded in the Torah. On the Jewish New Year called Rosh Hashana, pomegranates are eaten to wish for a year full of goodness.

The pomegranate is mentioned in the Torah, the Bible, and other ancient writings. The KJV Bible mentions pomegranate 25 times, and only in the Old Testament.

Some scholars believe this is the fruit that tempted Adam and Eve, and not an apple.

Note of Interests: The Pomegranate belongs to the family of flowering plants called Punicaceae, which become edible fruit. There are two species included in the Punicaceae family, which are Punica granatum, and Punica protopunica. The Punica protopunica is only grown on an island called Socotra, located in the Indian Ocean, and they are smaller, not as sweet, have pink flowers, and not red flowers like the Punica granatum.

The pomegranates are known by other names in other parts of the world. Here are some of the other names by which Punica granatum pomegranate is called.

1. Granado – Spanish
2. Dulim or Dulima – Persia
3. Granatapfel – Germany
4. Granaatappel – Dutch
5. Delima – Malaya, a country formerly in Southeast Asia
6. Melogranato – Italy
7. Gangsalan – Indonesia
8. Roma – Brazil
9. Granad – Guatemaia, a country in Central America
10. Limoni – Samoan, a country in the central South Pacific Ocean

According to ancient history, the rinds of the pomegranate fruits were used to dye clothing and tan morocco leather.

The seeds and the juice from the seeds have been used for medical purposes for hundreds of years.

According to the Bible, the pomegranate symbolizes spirituality, fertility, and love. The Catholic church believes that the pomegranate fruit symbolizes eternal life and the resurrection of Jesus Christ from the grave. The pomegranate is mentioned by name in the Bible, and several are listed below.

1.   The Promised Land for Israel was to be one of wheat, and barley, and vines, and fig trees and pomegranates; a land of oil olive, and honey, Deuteronomy 8:8.
2.   The garment of the High Priest had embroidered pomegranates of blue, purple, and scarlet woven around the hem of the robe, with bells of gold between them, Exodus 28:33 – 34.

Question: Who was the first group of High Priests? *Smile*

The answer is in the back of the book

1.   A_____
2.   Na_____
3.   Ab_____
4.   Eleazar
5.   I_____

3.   The 12 spies Moses sent out to spy out the Promised Land, cut down a branch with a single cluster of grapes so large that it took 2 men to carry the branch. They also brought back pomegranates and figs from the valley of Eshcol, Numbers 13:17 – 23.

4. The Israelites complained to Moses that the desert of Zin didn't have seed, figs, vines, pomegranates, or water to drink, Numbers 20:1 – 5.

5. Saul and his 600 men were camped on the outskirts of Gibeah under a pomegranate tree at Migron, preparing for battle against the Philistines, 1 Samuel 14.

6. King Solomon sent for a man named Hiram, who lived in Tyre. Hiram was a skillful bronze builder. King Solomon had Hiram to come to Jerusalem to make bronze furnishing for the LORD's Temple. Hiram made two bronze pillars, which were 27 feet tall, and 6 feet across. On the top of each pillar, he made a bronze cap 7 ½ feet high. The pillar caps were decorated with seven rows of chains and two rows of bronze pomegranates. The two pillars were placed on each side of the main door of the Temple, 1 Kings 7:13 – 21.

Question: What was the name of the two pillars at the main door of the Temple?

The answer is in the back of the book

_____

_____

7. Hiram completed everything King Saul had assigned him to make for the Temple of God, which included 400 pomegranates that hung from the chains on the caps that decorated the temple's pillars, 1 Kings 7:42 and 2 Chronicles 4:13.

8. Solomon likened the cheeks of his beloved to rosy pomegranates behind her veil, Song of Solomon 4:3 and 6:7.

Your cheeks are like rosy pomegranates behind your veil.
Song of Solomon 6:7 NLT

9. A bride's beauty is described as an orchard of pomegranates with precious fruits, henna with spikenard plants, Song of Solomon 4:13.
10. Song of Solomon 7:12 reads, "Let us get up early and go to the vineyards to see if the grapevines have budded, if the blossoms have opened, and if the pomegranates have bloomed. There I will give you my love." NLT
11. According to Song of Solomon 8:2, the juice from the pomegranate could be made into a spiced wine.

**I would lead you and bring you to my mother's house
– she who has taught me.
I would give you spiced wine to drink,
the nectar of my pomegranates.**
Song of Solomon 8:2 NIV

12. The pomegranate tree withering is mentioned among the judgment of God against the children of Israel, Joel 1:12.

**The vine is dried up and the fig tree is withered;
the pomegranate, the palm and the apple tree
– all the trees of the field – are dried up.
Surely the people's joy is withered away.**
Joel 1:12 NIV

13. The LORD promises a blessing to Israel through the Prophet Haggai on the 24th day of the 9th month. The LORD said he would allow the vine, the fig tree, the pomegranate, and the olive tree to produce, again, Haggai 2:10 – 19.

CHAPTER 3
INVERTED FLOWERS

According to Genesis 3:7, Adam and Eve sewed leaves from a fig tree together and made themselves aprons in the Garden of Eden. The figs on a fig tree are really flowers. The fig is an arrangement of multiple flowers turned inwards, with many tiny flowers arranged on the inside of the fig. The flowers of the fig are not seen until the fig is slice open. The figs are considered an eatable inverted flower, which eventually turns into the fruit that is eaten. The fruits can be eaten either ripe or dried.

The figs are uniquely pollinated by very tiny fig wasps that crawl through the opening in search of a place to lay eggs. The wasp, in turn, pollinates the flower with pollen. When the wasp dies, it is broken down by enzymes inside the fig and dissolved. The dissolved wasp inside the flower will not transmit any harmful disease or side effects to humans when they eat the figs. If this process does not take place, the fig trees could not reproduce.

Note of Interests: If the fig is a male, the fig wasp lays her eggs inside of the fig, and these eggs will hatch into larvae that burrow out and become wasps and fly off. If the wasp climbs into a female fig, the kind people eat, the fig wasp pollinates it, but cannot lay her eggs and dies.

The Common Fig scientific name is "Ficus carica," which is an Asian species of flowering plants in the Mulberry family, known as the "common fig" or "fig." These figs grow in warm climates, and depending on the type of fig trees, each fig fruit can contain up to several thousand seeds. Figs have been used for food and made into medicine. Figs contain vitamin A, vitamin C, sugars, and enzymes. It has been used as a laxative since ancient times, but the fig sap has been known to irritate the skin and eyes.

Note of Interests: There are over 700 varieties of fig trees, separated into 4 main groups, which are Caprifig, Smyrna, San Pedro, and Common Fig. Common Fig trees are the most popular and can grow to heights up to 30 feet. The Common Fig trees were one of the 1st plants that were cultivated, dating back to 9200 BCE. They were discovered in the early Neolithic village Gilgal I in the Jordan Valley, north of Jericho. According to Joshua 5:9, Gilgal is the camp where Joshua and the children of Israel settled first upon entering the Promised Land.

The "fig tree leaves" are mentioned first, and only once in the Bible. The fig tree is the 3rd tree mentioned in the Bible, indirectly. The other two trees are the Tree of Life, and the 2nd tree is called the Tree of the Knowledge of Good and Evil, Genesis 3:7. The fig tree is the only tree specified for sure was in the Garden of Eden because Adam and Eve made clothes for themselves from the large leaves of the fig tree, Genesis 3:6 – 7.

And the eyes of them both (Adam and Eve) **were opened,
and they knew they were naked; and
they sewed fig leaves together,
and made themselves aprons.**
Genesis 3:7 KJV

The word "fig(s)" is mentioned approximately 46 times in the KJV Bible, in relation to leaves, tree(s), and the fig fruit. The Common Fig tree has a short solid trunk with thick branches and the twigs bearing coarsely rough leaves. The roundish fruits called figs ripen to a purplish-brown color on the inside, and a greenish-brown color on the outside, during the summer.

In biblical days, figs were a crucial part of the Israelite diet. The fig trees of Palestine, whose scientific name is Fiscus carica will produce figs twice and sometimes 3 times in a year. The early-ripe figs ripen at the end of June. The summer fig then begins to form and ripen around August. The 3rd crop of figs is called green figs or winter figs, which will mature in a sheltered location.

The fig represented prosperity, well-being, security, and blessing, 1 Kings 4:25, Micah 4:4, Zechariah 3:10.

**In that day each of you
will invite your neighbor to sit under
your vine and fig tree,
declares the LORD Almighty.**
Zechariah 3:10 NIV

In Jeremiah's prophecy concerning the Judean exiles who were taken to Babylon, the LORD used "two baskets of figs" as an illustration in Jeremiah 24. One basket was filled with fresh ripe figs, while the other basket was filled with rotten figs that could not be eaten.

The LORD told Jeremiah, the good figs means He would send Judah to the land of Babylonians, but would watch over them, and care for them, and later bring them back to their land. The bad figs represent the King Zedekiah of Judah, his officials, all the people left in Jerusalem, and those who live in Egypt. The Lord told Jeremiah he would make them an object of horror; they will be scattered, disgraced, mocked, and cursed.

The Bible also uses the word "fig" with cake. Dried figs were pressed together and made into cakes. According to 1 Samuel 25:18, Abigail the wife of Nabal, took 200 loaves of bread, 2 skins of wine, 5 sheep ready for cooking, 5 seahs of roasted grain, 100 raisin cakes, and 200 fig cakes to David and his soldiers.

According to 1 Samuel 30:12, when David's soldiers found an Egyptian in the countryside, they brought him to David. He was given bread to eat, a piece of fig cake, 2 raisin cakes, and water.

In the New Testament, Jesus refers to figs and figs trees several times. In the Gospel of Matthew 7:15 – 20, Jesus spoke about watching out for false prophets. He stated that a good tree produces good fruit, and every rotten tree produces bad fruit. Jesus asked the question, do people pick a bunch of grapes from thorny weeds, or do they get figs from thistles? Jesus is referring to being able to identify a false prophet.

In the Gospel of Luke 21:29 – 33, Jesus gives a parable using a fig tree as a demonstration. Jesus said that when a fig tree sprout leaves, we know that summer is near, and in the same way, we shall know that destruction is near when nations and kingdom fight against each other; when there are earthquakes and widespread famines and epidemics.

In the Gospel of Mark 11:12 – 21, Jesus cursed a fruitless fig tree after leaving Bethany with his disciples.

In the Gospel of John 1:45 – 51, Jesus told Nathaniel before his brother, Philip, called him; he saw him sitting under a fig tree.

The fig tree is mentioned by Jesus in recognizing the signs of the times in Matthew 24:32 – 35, and then again in Revelation 6:12 – 17.

Note of Interests: Another kind of fig tree is the Sycamore, and its scientific name is Ficus sycomorus, also known as a fig-mulberry tree. The Sycamore fig trees grew in Egypt and warmer areas of Israel. This large tree usually has low-growing branches, which would have enabled the short Zacchaeus to climb, to see Jesus, who was passing along the road of Jericho, Luke 19:4.

CHAPTER 4

THORNS AND THISTLES

According to Genesis 3, after Adam and Eve disobeyed God by eating from the Tree of Knowledge, the LORD cursed the ground with "thorns and thistles."

**It will produce thorns and thistles for you,
and you will eat the plants of the field.**
Genesis 3:18 WEB

Israel is still flourishing with these beautifully prickly weeds; they are everywhere, the roadsides, mountain hills, fields, meadows, pastures, and miles of open territory. These colorful thistles are considered very stubborn weeds by some people. The ancient herbalist will tell you that thistles have medicinal powers. The birdwatchers will say, if you plant thistles, they will attract birds and woodpeckers that dine on thistle seeds.

Thistle is the general name for a group of flowering plants that have leaves with sharp prickles on the stem, mostly in the family Asteraceae. The common name for some of the flowering plants in the Asteraceae family is listed below.

1. Carduus – about 127 species in the genus
2. Carlina – honors the Holy Roman Emperor Charles V
3. Carthamus – the Safflower is the best-known species is this class
4. Cicerbita – the flowerhead has 5 to 30 florets

5. Cirsium – is also known as the common and field thistle

6. Cnicus – the flowers are yellow with a dense flowerhead

7. Cynara – the flowering plant is in the sunflower family

8. Echinops – is commonly known as Globe thistle, in the Daisy family

9. Notobasis – Syrian thistle is the other name, the flower is purple

10. Onopordum – is known as the Cotton, Scots, and Scotch thistle

11. Scolymus – is assigned to the Daisy family, with a yellow flowerhead

12. Silybum – Common name is Milk thistle, has purple flowers and white veins

13. Sonchus – Common name is Sow thistle; flowerhead is yellow

The tumbleweed and prickly poppy are sometimes called thistles, but they are not in the family of Asteraceae.

Note of Interests: Tumbleweed and the prickly poppy are plants that are sometimes thought of as thistles, but they are not. Prickly poppies are a flowering plant in the family Papaveraceae, and there are over 32 species. The tumbleweed is any of several plants, abundant in grassland, flatland, lowland, and meadows that breaks from the root plants at maturity. The tumbleweeds form into a large round tangle of hardened twigs that is blown by the wind. As the wind blows the tumbleweeds, they scatter seeds that have been trapped inside them.

————————◆◆◆◆◆————————

Thistles bloom in several colors, and there are several varieties. Israel has many types of thistles, mostly in the shades of pink and purple, but also come in bright yellow, and light purple. The following thistles cover the landscape of Israel at the brownest part of the dry season, Syrian, Spotted Golden, Artichoke, Holy Milk, and the Cherry Purple Globe.

However, the Bible refers to "thistles and thorns" as a symbol of desolation or wilderness. It is not possible to confirm which "thorns and thistles" God was referring to when he cursed the earth with "thorns and thistles," Genesis 3:17 – 18. Scholars believe that there are over 20 different words used for "thorny plants" in the Bible.

The Silybum marianum or Milk thistle is one of the thistles that has been present in Israel for thousands of years. The Milk thistles have both "spines and thorns." The prickle thorns help the plant from being eaten by animals. The plant originated from the mountains of the Mediterranean region. It will bloom from June to August in the North Hemisphere, and December to February in the Southern. The Milk thistle can adapt to dry, hot, and sunny areas, as well as wasteland. The Milk thistle is considered a troublesome invasive weed in most areas.

A single Milk thistle flowerhead can produce 100 – 200 seeds. The seeds have been known to lay dormant in the soil for many years until a rainfall. Once established, it can grow 2 – 6 feet tall with dense mass flower clumps that take the place of forage plants. Milk thistle accumulates nitrogen, and when ingested by animals can be toxic.

The scientific name for Milk thistle is Silybum marianum. The flowering plant is named for the white veins on its large prickly leaves. The Milk thistle is called by many names, and some are Cardus marianus, Blessed milk thistle, Marian thistle, Mary thistle, Saint Mary's thistle, Holy thistle, Lady's thistle, Mediterranean milk thistle, Scotch thistle, and Variegated thistle.

For over 2,000 years, around the world, the Milk thistle has been in humanity's diet and part of their medical remedies. All the parts of the Milk thistle plant can be used as food. The root of the Milk thistle can be eaten raw, or boiled, or roasted. The young plant's shoots in spring can be cut down to the root and eaten. The flower's stems can be stewed, after being peeled. The Milk thistle's leaves, once the prickles are trimmed off, can be boiled, or the leaves can be added raw to salads.

Milk thistle extracted will counteract mushroom poisoning, support the liver functions, increase the appetite, and aids in digestion. Milk thistle is a great tonic and can be used as an herbal tea to help the gallbladder.

Before Adam and Eve's sin, the earth contained only plants that were identified by God as good, attractive, and beneficial for man and animals to eat, Genesis 1:11 – 13. The whole world changed when Adam and Eve disobeyed God and stepped outside His will. God cursed the ground because of their disobedience, Genesis 3:17 – 19. In sorrow, Adam and Eve would painfully toil the food they would eat, as the soil grew thorns and thistles.

The plant botanist defines thorns as the sharp protuberance woody structure on a plant stem or vine. The Notobasis syriaca, also called the Syrian thistle, is a species in the thistle family of Asteraceae. Scholars believe that it could have been the "thorns" that suffocated the grain in Jesus' parable concerning the farmer sowing seed in Matthew 13:1 - 23.

Other seed fell among thorns, which
grew up and choked the plants.
Still other seed fell on good soil,
where it produced a crop
– a hundred, sixty or thirty times what was shown.
Matthew 13:7 – 8 NIV

Scholars believe the Syrian thistle might as well have been those that Gideon used as a whip concerning the biblical event with Zebah and Zalmunna, Judges 8:1 – 21.

So Gideon said,
"After the LORD gives me victory
over Zebah and Zalmunna,
I will return and tear your flesh
with the thorns and briers
from the wilderness."
Judges 8:7 NLT

PS: In the above verse, Gideon was speaking to the officials of Succoth, who refused to give his warriors some food, when Gideon and his 300 men were chasing Zebah and Zalmunna, the kings of Midian, Judges 8:4 – 6.

**Gideon then returned to Succoth and said to the leaders,
"Here are Zebah and Zalmunna.
When we were here before, you taunted me,
saying 'Catch Zebah and Zalmunna first,
and then we will feed your exhausted army.'"
Then Gideon took the elders of the
town and taught them a lesson,
punishing them with thorns and
briers from the wilderness.**
Judges 8:15 – 16 NLT

Many Scholars believe the Sarcopoterium spinosum thistle to be the plant used for the "crown of thorns" placed on Jesus' head, Matthew 27:29. It is viewed as a lower growing shrub abundant around Jerusalem, blossom around March, until May with pink flowers. The Sarcopoterium spinosum has thorns up to 4 inches long, and it is flexible, which would have been easy to weave into a crown.

Other Scholars believe the "crown of thorns" were Ziziphus spina-christ, which is known as, a Christ's Thorn Jujube evergreen plant. It grows into a thick, tangled crown of thorns in Palestine's valleys, and produces small flowers that can be eaten as a ripened fruit. The flowers on the Christ's Thorn Jujube evergreen plants are yellow and green.

The Paliurus spina-christi is another low thorny perennial plant believed to be used by the Roman soldiers in making a "crown of thorns" for Jesus' head. The Paliurus spina-christi is also known as Jerusalem thorn, Christ's thorn, or crown of thorns, and it blooms yellow flowers in spring.

They braided a crown of thorns and put it on his head,
and a reed in his right hand;
and they kneeled down before him and mocked him,
saying,
"Hail, King of the Jews!"
Matthew 27:29 WEB

CHAPTER 5
OLIVE AND OLIVES

The Olive Tree, with its flowery berries, is believed to have been in the Garden of Eden, even though the Bible does not say, directly. In maturity, the Olive Tree can grow over 40 feet and produce up to 100 pounds of olives each season, while the dwarf and semi-dwarf species will produce up to 40 pounds of olives.

Scientists found fossil evidence that indicates the Olive Tree had its origins over 30 million years ago in the Eastern Mediterranean. The research revealed that Olive Trees could live as long as 1,500 years. Olives were first cultivated 7,000 years ago in the Mediterranean region. The Mediterranean region consists of the nations that surround the Mediterranean Sea. Spain, France, Monaco, Italy, Malta, Slovenia, Croatia, Bosnia, Montenegro, Albania, Greece, Turkey, Syria, Cyprus, Lebanon, Israel, Palestine Gaza Strip, Egypt, Libya, Tunisia, Algeria, and Morocco are some of the nations that border the Mediterranean Sea.

Question: How many of these nations can you recall mentioned in the Bible? *Smile The answer is in the back of the book*

Your answer?

1. Spain
2. _____
3. _M_____

4. _____

5. _____

6. Syria

7. _____

8. _____

9. _____

10. _____

11. _E_____

12. Libya

As far back as 3,000 years ago, olives were grown commercially in Crete and sold abroad. Olives are considered the fruits of the Olive Tree, blooming in spring with small whitish flowers in loose clusters on the axils of the leaves. Olives are classified as a fruit because they are formed from the ovary of the olive flower, which matures into an olive.

Olives are harvested in several stages, arranging from green in color to dark purple. The 2 types of olive flowers are called perfect and staminate. The perfect olive flowers contain both male and female parts, which are capable of developing olive fruits. The staminate flowers have only the pollen-producing male structure, and therefore, cannot produce fruits.

The word "olive" is mentioned 1st in the Book of Genesis, along with the word "leaf."

The dove Noah released from the Ark brought him an "olive leaf," in its beak. This was God's way of informing Noah that the land was again supporting plant life. It allowed Noah to know that the water was receding from the earth, Genesis 8:11. Seven days later, Noah sent the dove out the

Ark for the second time, but this time, it didn't return. Only then did Noah remove the covering of the Ark to look out, and he saw dry land. However, Noah remained on the Ark another 6 weeks before God allowed him to leave.

Genesis 8:11 is the only verse in the KJV Bible where the words "olive leaf" are mentioned together.

> **And the dove came in to him in the evening;**
> **and, lo, in her mouth was an olive leaf pluckt off:**
> **so Noah knew that the waters were**
> **abates from the earth.**
> Genesis 8:11 KJV

Note of Interests: Scholars believed that 1656 years separated the day God made Adam, and the day Noah entered the Ark, God told him to build.

The olives from the olive trees were one of the leading food sources for the ancient Israelites. The olive oil made from olives were used for daily nourishment, medical issues, anointing officials, and lighting lamps. The leaves on the branches of the olive trees were ritually offered to deities and used to crown the champion of friendly games, and conquerors of bloody wars.

Note of Interests: Scholars believe that the oil the five wise virgins and five foolish virgins had in their lamps were olive oil, Matthew 25:1 – 13. The five wise virgins made sure they had extra oil for their lamps as they waited for the bridegroom to come, but the five foolish virgins did not.

The five foolish virgins begged the wise ones for some oil, but the wise virgins could not spare any. While the five foolish virgins went to buy more oil, the bridegroom came, and they were denied entrance into the wedding feast when they returned.

———————◆◆◆◆———————

Since ancient times, olive oil has been considered sacred. In the Old Testament, olive oil was used as part of the sacrificial grain offering, and the anointing oil to anoint individuals for the priestly office, Leviticus 2, Exodus 30. According to 1 Samuel 1, kings were anointed with olive oil as a sign that they were chosen by God to reign. Olive oil was used for lighting the Temple's lamps, depending on its quality, and used to sanctify the tabernacles, and all its furnishing, Exodus 40.

The word "olive" without the (s) is mentioned in 30 verses, 31 times; twice in Deuteronomy 28:40. Beginning in Deuteronomy 28, Moses is telling the Israelites, the LORD's blessing for obeying his commands, and curses for disobeying it. Deuteronomy 28:40 is one of the curses for disobeying the LORD's commands, which "olive" is mentioned.

You will grow olive trees throughout your land,
but you will never use the olive oil, for
the fruit will drip before it ripens.
Deuteronomy 28:40 NLT

Question: What 2 mountains are the blessings and curses are to be read from?

Oh, yes, smile . . . The answer is in the back of the book

1. _____

2. _____

The Olive Tree is mentioned in the Old Testament concerning the parable of Jotham, Judges 9:7 – 21. In the New Testament, Paul's Epistle to the Romans uses the Olive Tree to refer to the scattering and gathering of Israel. Romans 11:17 and Romans 11:24, compare the Israelites to a tame Olive Tree and the Gentiles to a wild Olive Branch.

Olive oil is mentioned as one of the plentiful foods in the Promised Land, Deuteronomy 8:8. The books of Exodus and Leviticus speak of the olive oil for the Temple, and Temple's lights. According to Exodus 30:22 - 24, approximately one gallon of pure-beaten olive oil was used to make incense for the Temple, along with pure myrrh, cinnamon, calamus, and cassia.

Note of Interests: The myrrh, cinnamon, calamus, and cassia are all flowering plants. The myrrh is a small tree, which grows 5 to 15 feet tall. They are found on rocky hills and produces tiny white flowers, and the fragrant sap is extracted from under the tree bark. A cinnamon tree can grow up to 30 feet tall, which has clusters of very tiny star-shaped flowers covering the tree in spring, but the spice is made from the inner tree bark. The calamus is a reed-like plant that grows about 5 feet in swamps and very wet places. The calamus has white and green stripe leaves, with yellow flowers; the leaves give off the sweet scent. The cassia plant grows about 10 feet tall with bright yellow flowers approximately 2 inches wide, with dark green leaves.

⸺◆◈◆⸺

According to Job 15, Job's friend Eliphaz, answered him using the word "olive" as a figurative expression, in verse 33. It reads, "They will be like a vine whose grapes are harvested too early, like an olive tree that loses its blossoms before the fruit can form."

In the New Testament, the word "olive" without the (s) is only mentioned in 4 verses, but a total of 7 times: twice in Romans 11:17, and trice in Romans 11:24. In the books of Romans and Revelation, the word "olive" is referring to trees, but in the Book of James, he uses the word "olive" in conjunction with the word "berries."

> **Can the fig tree, my brethren, bear olive berries?**
> **Either a vine, figs?**
> **So can no fountain both yield salt water and fresh.**
> James 3:12 KJV

Now, the word "olives" with the "s" is mentioned 15 times in the KJV Bible, but only 4 times in the Old Testament, and twice in Zechariah 14:4. The New Testament mentioned "olives" with the (s) 11 times, in 11 verses and only in the gospel books of the Bible, Matthew, Mark, Luke, and John. The word "olives" in the gospel books is in conjunction with the "Mount of Olives. The Mount of Olives is referred to as "Olivet" in 2 Samuel 15:30 and Acts 1:12, and "the mount facing Jerusalem," in 1 Kings 11:7.

The Mount of Olives is holy to Judaism, Christianity, and Islam. The Mount of Olives in biblical days was covered with olive trees on its slopes. By DNA testing, several trees in the Garden of Gethsemane date back to the time of Jesus.

The Mount of Olives is a mountain ridge that runs approximately 2.2 miles east of the Old Jerusalem, separated from Jerusalem by the Kidron Valley, also called Jehoshaphat Valley. In the Old Testament, Mount of Olives is mentioned first in 2 Samuel 15:30, when David fled from his son, Absalom, "And David went up by the ascent of Mount of Olives and wept as he went up."

Zechariah 14:4 refers to Mount of Olives in the prophecy of the "end of days." He prophesied the LORD of hosts would "stand on the Mount of Olives," and the mount will split in half. According to 1 Kings 11:7 – 8, after King Solomon turned away from God, he built pagan altars on Mount of Olives for gods of foreign wives. According to Ezekiel 11:23, Ezekiel had a vision of the LORD's glory, leaving Jerusalem, but it stopped above the Mount of Olives on the east before leaving.

In the New Testament, the Mount of Olives is frequently mentioned. Jesus often traveled over the Mount of Olives on the 40-minute walk from the Temple to Bethany. Before the destruction of the Temple, the Mount of Olives was the place where many Jews slept, under the olive trees, during the time of pilgrimage.

The Mount of Olives is where Jesus prayed outside the city on the lower western slope of Mount of Olives. From the Mount of Olives, Jesus entered Jerusalem at the beginning of the last week of his life. He traveled down the Mount of Olive triumphant as he enters Jerusalem riding a donkey on Psalm Sunday, around 33 AD. As Jesus traveled down Mount of Olives, he wept over Jerusalem's future destruction, Matthew 21, Mark 11, and Luke 19.

Note of Interests: During the siege of Jerusalem, which led to the destruction of the city in 70 AD, Roman Soldiers camped on the Mount of Olives.

Two days before Jesus' Crucifixion, in his Olivet Discourse, he foretells the destruction of Jerusalem and the end of the world, Matthew 24 – 25; Mark 13; Luke 21. Jesus spoke to his disciples on the Mount of Olives foretelling his Second Coming, Matthew 24:27 – 31. The Garden of Gethsemane lies at the foot of the Mount of Olives. The New Testament tells how Jesus and his disciples sang together, Matthew 26:30. Jesus prayed there with his disciples the night before he was betrayed and arrested, Matthew 26:30 – 55.

Scholars believe that the Garden of Gethsemane, where Jesus prayed just before he was betrayed by Judas Iscariot, is on the western slopes of the Mount of Olives, Matthew 25, Mark 14.

Finally, after the Resurrection, Jesus is reported to have ascended into heaven from the Mount of Olives, Acts 1:9 – 12.

In Jewish tradition, the Messiah will descend the Mount of Olive on Judgment Day, and enter Jerusalem through the

Golden Gate, known as the "Beautiful Gate." Therefore, Jews have sought to be buried on the slopes of the Mount of Olives, which serves as one of Jerusalem's main cemeteries, with an estimated 150,000 graves. Among the catacombs contains the graves associated with Zechariah and Absalom, and on the upper slope are the "Tombs of the Prophets," Haggai, Zechariah, and Malachi who lived in the 6th and 5th BC.

Note of Interests: A joint mosque and Christian chapel exist over the spot where many Christians and Muslins believe Jesus ascended.

The books of Zechariah and Revelation are the only books in the Bible that have the phrase "two olive trees." In the Book of Zechariah, the angel of the LORD woke Zechariah from his sleep and asked him what he saw. Zechariah answered, "a candlestick of all gold, with a bowl upon the top of it, seven lamps, seven pipes, and "two olive trees" by it, one upon the right side of the bowl, and the other upon the left side thereof," in Zechariah 4:2 – 4 KJV. The two witnesses mentioned in Revelation 11:4 is spoken of as "two olive trees" standing before God.

> **These are the two olive trees,**
> **and the two candlesticks standing**
> **before the God of the earth.**
> Revelation 11:4 KJV

CHAPTER 6

MANDRAKES

The plant with the scientific name Mandragora autumnalis is known as "mandrakes" in the Bible. The Mediterranean plant has oval-shaped leaves arranged in a rosette that spread up to 2 feet across and grows remarkably close to the ground. The mandrake plants have bell-shaped purplish flowers in the winter, followed by yellow or orange berries in the summer. The "mandrake" is the root of the flowery plant, which grows 3 to 4 feet deep in the ground. The shapes of the mandrake roots often resemble 2 legs of humans.

Mandragora is a plant genus belonging to the Solanaceae family, and members of this genus are known as mandrakes. Scientists debate that there are between 3 to 5 species in the genus. It is believed that the 2 species located around the Mediterranean area are the mandrakes of ancient days. The other species are found in China. The mandrake has the reputation of being an aphrodisiac.

All mandragora are perennial herbaceous plants with deep sizeable taproots, grows close to the ground, and leaves develop into a circular arrangement. Herbaceous perennial plants do not have woody stems that will remain above the ground when their leaves die. When herbaceous plants withers and dies, they regrow back on their own during spring and summer. The herbaceous perennial plants have underground roots or bulbs that will survive the harsh winter months. The word "Herbaceous" in botany is frequently shortened to "herbs."

In biblical days, the mandrakes were associated with the superstitious belief that it promoted fertility and conception in barren women. The mandrakes root would be consumed in small amounts because the species of Mandragora contain active alkaloids that make the plants poisonous. The mandrake would also be cut into pieces and placed in an amulet to wear on the body or put beneath the bed to encourage conception.

The Bible mentioned "mandrakes" only in the books of Genesis and Song of Solomon. According to Genesis 29:13 – Genesis 30:22, Jacob was living with his mother's brother named Laban in Paddan Aram. Laban had two daughters that Jacob married. Jacob was tricked into marrying Leah, his 1st wife, who was older than her sister Rachel. Seven days later, Jacob married Rachel and agreed to work 7 more years for Laban for her. Jacob loved Rachel more than Leah.

In brief, Leah had birthed 4 sons by Jacob and stopped conceiving. Rachel had birthed Jacob, no children, but Jacob spent his nights with Rachel instead of Leah.

Leah's oldest son, Reuben, found mandrake flower plants in the field and brought them home to his mother. When Rachel saw the plants, she asked Leah for them.

Leah was resentful of Jacob's preference for Rachel, so Leah asked Rachel, "Wasn't it enough that you stole my husband?" will you take my son's mandrakes too?" Rachel responded by proposing a trade, Jacob can sleep with you tonight in return for the mandrakes, and eagerly Leah agreed.

When Jacob came home after being in the field, he was met by Leah, who said, "You must sleep with me. I hired you with my son's mandrake." Leah became pregnant and bore Jacob, a 5th son who was named Issachar. Then Leah became pregnant with a 6th son named Zebulun, and later a daughter named Dinah.

Rachel did not become pregnant after acquiring and using the mandrake. Rachel finally conceived after Leah had seven children by Jacob, 6 sons and one daughter.

Note of Interests: The majority of the Bible translations use the word "mandrakes." The CEB (Common English Bible) uses the words "erotic herbs" instead of the word "mandrakes." Other Bible translations also use other words instead of "mandrakes," and they are listed below.

1. YLT (Young's Literal Translation) uses the words "love-apples."
2. CEV (Contemporary English Version) uses the words "love flowers."
3. ERV (Easy to Read) uses the words "special flowers."
4. NLV (New Life Version) uses the word "fruit."

The mandrakes are mentioned once in the Song of Solomon. According to Solomon, the mandrakes send out their fragrance for his beloved.

**There are mandrakes gives off their fragrance,
and the finest fruits are at our door,
new delights as well as old,
which I have saved for you, my lover.**
Song of Solomon 7:13 NLT

CHAPTER 7
SOLD HIS BIRTHRIGHT

According to Genesis 25:27 – 34, Esau sold his birthright to his younger brother, Jacob, for some bread and a bowl of red lentil stew. Esau and Jacob were the twins of Isaac and Rebekah, and Isaac was 60 years old when they were born. The twins were the grandsons of Abraham and Sarah.

Esau was born first with his fraternal twin, Jacob following. When Esau was born, he was covered with baby-fine red hair over his entire body, and that's why his parents named him Esau. The name Esau means "hairy." Jacob was born with his hand holding on to Esau's heel, so they named him Jacob. The name Jacob means "follow after."

As Esau and Jacob grew, Esau became a rugged skillful hunter. However, Jacob had a quiet personality, preferring to stay at home. The father, Isaac, loved Esau, but Rebekah loved Jacob.

One day, Esau returned home, while his twin brother was making stew. Esau was extremely hungry and tired because he had been in the fields. He begged Jacob to give him some stew, but Jacob would only give Esau a bowl of red lentil stew in exchange for his birthright, and Esau agreed.

Since the time of Exodus, the birthright of the first son was incredibly important. The first-born son was viewed as one who was able to protect the family. He would be an individual revered by others, knowing how to judge what is right and wrong, and act accordingly. The first-born son was entitled to a double portion of the inheritance and had authority over the family matters if the father was deceased.

Note of Interests: According to the Talmud, Esau sold his birthright to Jacob, soon after their grandfather, Abraham died. Scholars believe Esau and Jacob would have been 15 years old.

Lens is a genus of the legume family, which are referred to as "lentils." Legumes are a class of plants that includes beans, peanuts, clovers, carobs, peas, chickpeas, lentils, and a few others. Legumes are mostly known for their edible seeds with a protective outer covering. Legumes are cultivated, primarily for human consumption, it is also used for livestock fodder and ground fertilizer. Len culinaris is the Latin name for Lentils or Lentiles (KJV).

Even though beans and lentils are both in the legume family, some people have classified lentils as a type of bean, meaning there is no difference between the lentils and beans. The beans genus is Phaseolus, whereas lentils genus is Len. Whether lentil is a different class of legume from a bean is a matter of an individual's interpretation.

Lentils are smaller than beans, and lentils lose their shape and become soft and pulpy when cooked. There are several types of lentils, the brown and green, red, black beluga, and French, also known as "Lentilles du Puy." Red lentil has been the favorite down through centuries.

Note of Interests: Here are other examples of people's different interpretations. A cucumber grows from a flower and bear seeds, which technically makes it a fruit; however, most people view it as a vegetable; likewise, for tomatoes, and eggplants, which are technically fruits, also.

Lentils are self-pollinating and grow about 16 inches tall. The flowering begins from the lowermost buds and gradually moves upward. The lentils have small whitish to light purple pea-like flowers. The flat roundish shaped seeds range in several colors and grow in a small pod, with at least 2 seeds in each pod.

Lentils are known as "pulse crops," and two other pulse crops in biblical days were broad beans (Vicia fabal), and the chickpea (Cicer arichinum). The word "pulse" comes from the Latin word "puls," which means thick soup. Lentils are the oldest pulse crop. Lentils with another pulse were used in Roman Catholic countries during Lent, and some scholars believe this is where the name "Len" originated.

Note of Interests: Scholars believe broad beans, chickpeas, and lentils were the foods that Daniel and his friends, Hananiah, Mishael, and Azariah, requested to eat in Babylon, Daniel 1:12.

Lentils are rich in fiber and proteins and have a good source of vitamins A and B, along with potassium and iron. Lentils also help with digestion, contain the essential amino acids, and electrolytes. Lentil seeds were commonly used in soups and stews, cooked into a thick gravy. Lentils can be made into flour by grinding uncooked lentils and baked into bread.

Lentils are spoken of 4 times in the Old Testament, only, and they are listed below.

Genesis 25:34

Jacob gave Esau bread and lentil stew. He ate and drank, rose up, and went his way. So, Esau despised his birthright. WEB

2 Samuel 17:28

They brought sleeping mats, cooking pots, serving bowls, wheat and barley, flour and roasted grains, beans, lentils. NLT

2 Samuel 23:11

Next to him was Shammah son of Agee the Hararite. When the Philistines banded together at a place where there was a field full of lentils, Israel's troops fled from them. NIV

Ezekiel 4:9

Take thou also unto thee wheat, and barley, and beans, and lentils, and millet, and fitches, and put them in one vessel, and make thee bread thereof, according to the number of the days that thou shalt lie upon thy side, three hundred and ninety days shalt thou eat thereof. KJV

CHAPTER 8

THE ROSE OF SHARON

In the ancient world, "rose of Sharon" was a rare rose that grew only on the peaks of mountains. It was considered a precious treasure, and to find it required climbing treacherous mountains at a high altitude. The rose of Sharon would bloom white, and as the rose of Sharon begins to age, it turns pinkish and then a dark red color, and afterward, it dies and falls to the ground, and then the flower bud next to it opens with a white bud. Ancient folklore connects the short life cycle of the blossoming roses on the rose of Sharon to the crucifixion, death, burial, and resurrection of Jesus.

The rose of Sharon blossoms into a trumpet-shaped flower, it has 5 large petals with a distinguished crown center. The flower is often crinkly that gives the notion they are made of delicate crepe paper. The leaves can be eaten raw, and they taste like lettuce. The rose of Sharon's leaves can also be brewed into a tea. The flowers are also edible and have a fruity, tart taste.

According to the dictionary, the "rose of Sharon" is described as a hardy plant of the mallow family with the name "Hibiscus syriarus." They have white, red, pink, or purplish flowers that blossom from mid-summer to late fall.

According to Wikipedia, the "rose of Sharon" is a common name that has been applied to several different species of flowering plants. The Sharon plain is one of the largest valley-plains in ancient Israel. The plain of Sharon was located along the Mediterranean Sea south of Mount

Carmel. It was 60 miles long and 10 miles wide. In the time of King Solomon, the plain of Sharon was extremely fertile and had many varieties of beautiful flowers and trees.

In the spring, the ground of Sharon's plains was covered with red roses, white lilies, scarlet tulips, yellow narcissus, anemones in its many colors, along with other flowers. Therefore, scholars believe that the rose of Sharon flower is named for the district of Sharon.

Note of Interests: The plain of Sharon is mentioned in Acts 9. Peter healed a man, living in Lydda named Aeneas, he had been paralyzed for 8 years. The people of Lydda and Sharon saw it and turned to the LORD, Acts 9:32 – 35.

Scholars have debated over what is the exact rose of Sharon flower mentioned in the Bible. The rose of Sharon bush has been suggested. Other scholars claim that the rose of Sharon was a tulip, known as the Sharon tulip. Others believe that the exact biblical rose of Sharon may have been one of these flowering plants.

1. Crocus
2. Madonna Lily
3. Narcissus Rose
4. Wild Hyacinth
5. Crown Daisy

The phrase "the rose of Sharon" is a biblical idiom of Jesus. There is only 1 reference to "the rose of Sharon" in the Bible, recorded in the Old Testament. The phrase "the rose of Sharon" goes hand-in-hand with "the lily of the valleys." There are several interpretations concerning Jesus, "the rose of Sharon," and "a lily of the valleys."

I am a rose of Sharon, a lily of the valleys.
Song of Solomon 2:1 WEB

One of the interpretations by scholars is that "the rose of Sharon" is a picture of Jesus. The rose flower only blooms on a high mountain top. Jesus blossomed from the top of a mountain called Calvary. The cross from which Jesus hung was like a blooming rose, and anyone who climbs the mountain will find the precious gift of salvation.

Another interpretation compares "the lily of the valleys" to "the rose of Sharon." The rose of Sharon is found on a mountain top compared to the lily of the valleys that are found in low places. The mountain tops and the valley lows are two extreme locations, but Jesus is both God of the mountains and the valleys.

Some Bible expositors view "the rose of Sharon," as Christ, and "the lily of the valley," as the church. The phrase "the rose of Sharon," exemplify the Savior, Jesus Christ, the King of Kings, in the beauty of a rose, and the sweetness of its fragrance. The fragrant rose flower comes forth from the clusters of outer leaves, with a crown in the center.

It has been expressed that "the rose of Sharon," is like Nazareth. Nazareth is the city where Jesus was raised by his parents, Mary and Joseph. The reason Nazareth is viewed as "the rose of Sharon" is because Nazareth is surrounded by mountains, as the rose of Sharon is surrounded by its leaves.

CHAPTER 9
LILIES

Lilium is a member of the true lilies, which can produce flower clusters up to 20 blossoms per stem and can grow up to 6 feet tall. There are many other plants that have "lily" as part of their common name but are not related to the true lilies. The daylilies, flame lilies, lily of the valley, and water lilies are flowers commonly referred to as lilies, but they are not in the genus Lilium.

The Latin name for true lilies is Lilium candidum, known as the Madonna lily. It is native to the Balkans and the Middle East. It has been cultivated for over 3,000 years. The true lilies are a genus of herbaceous flowering plants that grow from underground bulbs with large prominent trumpet-shaped flowers. Lilies are perennial flowers with a strong sweet-smelling fragrance, exceptionally beautiful, and its whiteness exceed all other flowers for whiteness, and within each lily are several gold anthers.

Lilies have great symbolic values for many cultures and have been important for centuries around the world. According to the ancient writer Pliny, lilies are the tallest flowers and hangs it trumpet-shaped flower blossom downward, depicting the beauty of the Son of God, showing His humility.

**Though he was God,
he did not think of equality with God
as something to cling to.**

**Instead, he gave up his divine privileges;
he took the humble position of a slave
and was born as a human being.
When he appeared in human form,
he humbled himself in obedience to God and
died a criminal's death on a cross.**
Philippians 2:6 – 8 NLT

Ancient folklores connected the lilies with motherhood. In early painting, the Angel Gabriel is seen handing a bouquet of white lilies to the Virgin Mary. In one legend, three days after the burial of Mary, when her tomb was visited, there was nothing in the tomb, except large bunches of lovely lilies.

Lilies have many healing qualities. According to ancient beliefs, lilies could be used to restore a lost voice, was good for the liver, and helped heal individuals with dropsy.

The Easter Lily's Latin name is Lilium longiforum, and the "true lily," Latin name is Lilium candidum. The Easter Lily has become the traditional flower of Easter and symbolizes "the resurrection" of Jesus. The beautiful white lily also represents purity, life, innocence, and hope to others.

The lilies are mentioned 10 times in the KJV Bible in both the Old and New Testament. They are mentioned the most in the Book of Song of Solomon. According to the verses listed below, some points can be made about the lilies in the Bible. They grow in the valleys and the fields, and many even grow among thorns. In speaking of God's blessing on Israel, Hosea stated that "he shall grow as the lily." The lily, with its beauty and lovely shape, was the architectural ornament of the Solomon's Palace, and the Temple in Jerusalem on Mount Moriah, 1 Kings 7, 2 Chronicles 4.

Hiram Makes the Bronze Furnishings for Solomon's Palace, 1 Kings 7:1 - 40

And it was an hand breadth thick, and the brim thereof was wrought like the brim of a cup, with flowers of lilies: it was contained two thousand baths, 1 Kings 7:26.

The Furnishings for the Temple, 2 Chronicles 4:1 – 22

And the thickness of it was an handbreadth, and the brim of it like the work of the brim of a cup, with flowers of lilies; and it received and held three thousand baths, 2 Chronicles 4:5.

Note of Interests: Scholars believe that the Lotus of Nile, also called a water lily, is the one mentioned in 1 Kings 7:26 and 2 Chronicles 4:5. When the water rises and all the fields are flooded, there appears above the surface a flowering plant, which the Egyptians called the Blue Lotus. The Lotus Flowers are cut down, dried in the sun, and the flower seeds are bake or made into bread. The large underground roots of the Lotus Flowers are eatable, also.

The Book of Song of Solomon uses the word "lilies" in several verses. The Book of Song of Solomon is a love poem written by Solomon during his reign 970 – 930 BC. It is a dialogue between a bridegroom and his bride, who are in love with each other. The bridegroom and bride use the word "lilies" in their conversation with each other, and they are listed below.

She Speaks, Song of Solomon 2:16

My beloved is mine, and I am his: he feedeth among the lilies.

He Speaks, Song of Solomon 4:5

Thy breasts are like two young roes that are twins, which feed among the lilies.

She Speaks, Song of Solomon 5:13

His cheeks are as a bed of spices, as sweet flowers: his lips like lilies, dropping sweet smelling myrrh.

She Speaks, Song of Solomon 6:2

My beloved I gone down into his garden, to the beds of spices, to feed in the gardens, and to gather lilies.

Scholars believe the lilies mentioned in the New Testament may be the brilliant red flowers that are abundant in Galilee. The lilies of the valley in the heights of Beersheba have grass and low shrubs growing between them. When camels graze in the fields and valleys, they will eat the twigs, stems, plant sprouts, and even the thorny plants, which most animals ignore. However, the camels will not touch the lilies; the camels will pull up and eat what lay between them.

Scholars believe when Jesus preached on a mountainside that was covered with thousands of wildflowers, is where the words "consider the lilies" originated from because of the beautiful wildflowers that were at His feet, Matthew 6 and Luke 12.

Jesus said, "Why Worry?" Matthew 6:25 – 34

And why take ye thought for raiment? Consider the lilies of the field, how they grow; they toil not, neither do they spin. And yet I say unto you, That even Solomon in all his glory was not arrayed like one of these. Wherefore, if God so clothe the grass of the field, which to day is, and to morrow is cast into the oven, shall he not much more clothe you, O ye of little faith? Matthew 6:28 - 30

Jesus said to His Disciple, "Don't Worry," Luke 12:22 – 31

Consider the lilies how they grow: they toil not, they spin not; and yet I say unto you, that Solomon in all his glory was not arrayed like one of these. If then God so clothe the grass, which is to day in the field, and to morrow is cast into the oven; how much more will he clothe you, O ye of little faith? Luke 12:27 – 28

CHAPTER 10

A TENTH

**Woe to you, teachers of the law and
Pharisees, you hypocrites!
You give a tenth of your spices
– mints, dill, and cumin.
But you have neglected the more
important matters of the law
– justice, mercy and faithfulness.
You should have practiced the latter, without
neglecting the former. Matthew 23:23 NIV**

In the Gospel of Matthew, chapter 23, Jesus criticized the religious leaders. He warned the teachers of the law of Moses and Pharisees against hypocrisy. Matthew 23:13 – 36 is where Jesus stated 7 woes to the teachers of the law and the Pharisees, and they are listed below.

The First Woe, Matthew 23:13

The religious leaders shut the door of the kingdom of heaven in the people's faces and would not allow the people who are trying to enter the kingdom of heaven, enter.

The Second Woe, Matthew 23:15

The religious leaders traveled over land and sea, misleading new converts.

The Third Woe, Matthew 23:16 – 22

The religious leaders gave false and misleading statements to the people concerning swearing by the Temple and altar.

The Fourth Woe, Matthew 23:23

The religious leaders tithed with mint, dill, and cumin, but refused to show justice, mercy, and faithfulness to the people.

The Fifth Woe, Matthew 23:25 – 26

The religious leaders appeared righteous on the outer appearance, but inwardly they are corrupt filled with greed and self-indulgence.

The Sixth Woe, Matthew 23:27 - 28

The religious leaders looked like beautiful whitewashed tombs on the outside, but they are overflowing with hypocrisy and wickedness.

The Seventh Woe, Matthew 23:29 - 36

The religious leaders honored the dead prophets by building tombs but murder the living prophets.

The 4th woe to the Pharisees and teachers of the law is Matthew 23:23. According to Jesus in Matthew 23:23, giving a tenth of your earning even down to the smallest things like mints, dill, and cumin is a good thing. However, Jesus also said in this verse, that the teachers of the law and Pharisees had neglected important matters like justice, mercy, and faithfulness. In Jesus' days, the Jews were required to tithe, which was a tax to support the Temple.

Note of Interests: The KJV Bible used the word "anise" instead of "dill," and the word "cumin" is spelled "cummin." In the KJV Bible, the phrase "teachers of the law" is replaced with the word "scribes."

From ancient times, mints, dill, and cumin have been used in medicine, and for flavoring food. Today, mint along with dill and cumin grows wild in Israel, mint being the most common. Mint and dills are considered an herb, and cumin is a spice.

Mint is a popular herb with more than 600 species. In biblical times, the Jews would scatter the synagogue floors with mint leaves so that the fragrance would saturate the air with each footstep. It was believed that the sweet-smelling fragrant would purify the temple crowd and protect against diseases. Dill leaves are widely used as herbs, while the flat oval tan dill seeds make it a spice. Cumin is a spice made from the dried seeds of the flowering plant and is a popular spice used in the cuisines of Mexico, Asia, the Mediterranean, and the Middle East.

Note of Interests: The difference between herbs and spices, the leaves of a plant make up the herbs, but spices come from seeds, roots, bulb, or stem bark of the plant. Herbs are used after drying, some herbs are used fresh, and spices are always dried before being used. Herbs and spices both have medicinal benefits, but herbs have more therapeutic benefits than spices. Herbs and spices are both used for adding flavor and aroma to food. Many herbs are used in the makeup creams and cosmetics, while some spices are used as preservatives.

The Latin name for mint is Mentha longifolia, also known as horsemint. Horsemint is believed by many Jewish scholars to be the mint Jesus is referring to in His discourse with the Pharisees, Matthew 23:23, Luke 11:42.

Jesus' discourse with the Pharisees of hypocrisy is recorded in Matthew, and then again in the Gospel of Luke, and mint is the one herb mentioned by both. In fact, mint is only mentioned twice in the KJV.

Matthew's gospel reads, **"Woe unto you, scribes and Pharisees, hypocrites! For ye pay tithe of mint and anise and cummin, and have omitted the weightier matters of the law, judgment, mercy, and faith: these ought ye to have done, and not to leave the other undone."** Mathew 23:23 KJV

Luke's gospel reads, **"But woe unto you, Pharisees! for ye tithe mint and rue and all manner of herbs, and pass over judgment and the love of God: these ought ye to have done, and not to leave other undone."** Luke 11:42 KJV

In Israel, there are many varieties of mint, but the horsemint is the most common.

The horsemint has been confused with Mentha spicata, which is spearmint. The horsemint is much larger than the other mints and grows over 3 feet tall, having tiny flowers in the color of pink, lilac, purple or white. Mints grow in moist, sunny places, where it tends to run wild. Horsemint still grows in Israel, between the Dead Sea and the Jordan River, especially the area surrounding Jerusalem. Horsemint is cultivated at Aleppo in Syria, which lies about 60 miles from the Mediterranean Sea on the west and 60 miles from the Euphrates River on the east.

Mint herbs were spread out in the homes of the Hebrews, and the Temple because of its clean and aromatic scent. Wild mint was a popular seasoning herb, and Jewish Leaders gave it as tithes to the Temple. Mint was served at the Spring Passover Feast of the Paschal Lamb.

**And God said,
Let the earth bring forth grass,
the herb yielding seed,
and the fruit tree yielding fruit after his kind,
whose seed is in itself, upon the earth: and it was so.**
Genesis 1:11 KJV

Note of Interests: In Greek mythology, Mintha was a river nymph. She was loved by the underworld god, Pluto, and became his concubine. When Mintha claimed to be superior to his wife, Persephone, she transformed Mintha into dust, from which Pluto caused the mint plant to grow.

The Latin name for dill is Anethum graveolens. The dill is also referred to as "anise" in KJV translation and only mentioned once. The name "anise" is derived from the Old French from Latin word "anisum," or Greek, anison, referring to dill.

The dill flowers are either white or yellow, approximately 1/8 inch in diameter produced in dense umbels. The plant grows up to 3 feet or taller. The leaves at the base of the plant are around 2 inches long; the leaves that are higher on the stems are feathery like on a stem. The fruit is an oblong dry schizocarp about ¼ inch long, usually called aniseed. A schizocarp is a dry fruit that matures, spit-up into mericarps.

Dill tends to replant itself and spread widely. When a dill blooms, its yellow-green flowers, it signals the end of the plant's life. Dill is cultivated for its aromatic seeds as a spice for flavoring foods, and as medicine for treating stomach ailments.

Note of Interests: Dill was thought to help defend against witchcraft.

The Latin name for Cumin is Cuminum cyminum. Cumin and Dill, like coriander, are members of the parsley family with spicy seeds. The cumin plant is best known for its spicy aromatic seeds, used in flavoring bread, cakes, stews, pastries, and liquors.

Note of Interests: Coriander (Coriandrum sativum) only mentioned twice in the KJV provided both tastily leaves and spicy seeds, while the Israelites were in the wilderness, Exodus 16:31, Numbers 11:7.

The cumin plant is an annual herbaceous plant that grows approximately 2 feet tall with slender, branched stem, about 11 inches long, and the leaves are about 3 inches long, harvested by hand. It is a short-lived flower that produces clusters of the cumin seed.

The cumin flowers are small, white, or pink in color. The cumin seeds are oblong in shape, about an inch long, mostly brownish-yellow in color.

Cumin has many health benefits. It helps to fight the flu, boosts the immune system, promotes a healthy digestive system, used as a diuretic, stimulates menstrual cycle in women, and kills intestinal worms, just to name a few.

Cumin is mentioned 4 times in the KJV Bible, 3 times in Isaiah 28, verses 25, 27, and 28. Isaiah 28:23 – 29, is concerning "How God Plants, Plows and Harvest." The best-known reference to cumin is in Matthew 23:23, when Jesus said, "Woe to you, teachers of the Law and Pharisees!" The "teachers of the Law" is also known as "scribes," the Jewish Leaders in the New Testament.

CHAPTER 11
TOXIC OLEANDER

The oleander is a gorgeous plant but is also toxic to humans and animals. All parts of the plant are poisonous, the plant sap causes skin irritation, touching the plant with bare hands can induce poisoning, and inhaling smoke from a burning oleander creates terrible side effects. The typical symptoms of oleander poisoning include arrhythmia, diarrhea, dizziness, seizures, and vomiting.

Oleander grows as a shrub along riverbanks, and some grow as a small tree and can tolerate long season of drought. There are over 300 varieties of oleander cultivated as decorative plants, rather than food, herb, or spice. The most popular oleanders are Algiers, Calypso, Hardy Red, Petite Salmon, and Sister Agnes.

The oleander plant can grow over 19 feet tall and bloom from summer to fall with fragrant flowers. The funnel-shaped flowers grow in clusters at the end of each branch in the color of reddish-brown, pink, lilac, red, purple, light-yellow, and white. The flowers are between 1 – 2 inches in diameter with 5 petals. The oleander plant produces a fruit, which is called a capsule, and each capsule contains many soft fluffy seeds.

The Oleander originated in the Middle East, and on Israel riverbanks, the rosy-colored flowers grow wild, displaying a beautiful layer of color over the outer edge of many lakes, ponds, and rivers. The Nerium oleander is a feature in many of the Roman wall paintings in Pompeii.

Note of Interests: Oleander was the first plant to blossom after the havoc of the atomic bomb in 1945.

Nerium oleander is the Latin name for oleander. The oleander is not explicitly mentioned in the Bible, but there are several beliefs concerning oleanders. Scholars believe the Nerium oleander was used to sweeten the bitter waters in Exodus 15:22 – 27. Moses had brought Israel across the Red Sea. The Israelites had been in the Wilderness of Shur for 3 days and found no water to drink. When the Israelites finally found some water in the wilderness, they could not drink the water because it was bitter. Moses cried out to the LORD and cast a tree into the water; the water was then made sweet.

> **And he (Moses) cried unto the LORD;**
> **and the LORD shewed him a tree,**
> **which when he had cast into the waters,**
> **the waters were made sweet:**
> **there he made for them a statute and an ordinance,**
> **and there he proved them.**
> Exodus 15:25 KJV

Question: The place where the bitter waters were found, what was it later named? _____

smile time . . . . The answer is in the back of the book

The "Rose of Jericho" is thought to refer to the oleander by some scholars. However, in traditional beliefs, the "Rose of Jericho" is a "tumbleweed," which blossom during the rainy winter season. When Jesus was led by the Spirit into the desert for 40 days and 40 nights, God sent what appears to be lifeless tumbleweeds to Jesus' feet, and it followed Him during his days in the desert. The tumbleweeds collected moisture from the night dew, and Jesus would quench his thirst from drops of water within the curved dry branches of the plants. The "Rose of Jericho" is also called the "Resurrection Plant."

The oleander by other scholars is believed to be the tree planted by the streams of water, which bring forth his fruit in due seasons in Psalm 1.

That person is like a tree planted by streams of water,
which yields its fruit in season and
whose leaf does not wither
– whatever they do prospers.
Psalm 1:3 NIV

Even though the oleander seeds and leaves are known to be toxic, they are used to make medicine. The medical use of the oleander plant dates back at least 3500 years. In 15th BC, the Mesopotamians believed in the healing powers of the oleander. The Babylonians treated hangovers by drinking oleander and licorice together. In 8th AD, the Arab's physicians were the 1st to treat cancer with oleander. Oleander extract is also used to treat heart conditions, asthma, epilepsy, leprosy, malaria, ringworms, warts, and venereal diseases. Hindu used the blooms of oleanders as funeral flowers.

Note of Interests: In the book titled Ivanhoe, written by Sir Walter Scott, it is believed that oleander soup, is the magic healing potion that Rebecca made to heal the injured Ivanhoe. When witchcraft accusation was brought against her, Ivanhoe came to her aid. Ivanhoe fights Bois-Guilbert, the Knight, for Rebecca's release, and emerges victorious over him.

CHAPTER 12

THE GIFTS

The Magi opened their treasures and presented gold, frankincense, and myrrh as gifts to the young child, Jesus. The Bible does not tell the exact age of Jesus at this time. However, scholars believe Jesus was about 2 years old when the 3 Magi visited Him. The Bible does not give a specific country from where the 3 Magi journeyed from to see Jesus over 2,000 years ago. Many scholars also believe there were more than 3 Magi, but many assumed there was 3 Magi because the Bible records the 3 types of gifts given to the young child, Jesus.

The Bible records that the Magi came from the "East." A group of wise men, also known as Magi, traveled from the "East" to search for the young child who had been born King of the Jews, Matthew 2:2. A star guided the wise men, and when they found the young child, they worshipped Him.

After Jesus was born in Bethlehem in Judea,
during the time of King Herod,
Magi from the east came to Jerusalem and asked,
"Where is the one who has been born king of the Jews?
We saw his star when it rose and
have come to worship him."
Matthew 2:1 – 2 NIV

Many scholars believe the Magi traveled east from Persia between 400 to 700 miles one-way, on camels. The areas of northern Arabia, Syria, and Mesopotamia are considered the "East" by Jews. In the Old Testament, there are several references to the location "East," which are listed below.

1. The city of Haran was located in "the land of the people of the east," Genesis 29:1.
2. The king of Moab summoned Balaam "from Aram," which is Syria, out of the mountains of the east, Numbers 23:7.
3. The prophet Isaiah spoke of Cyrus, the Persian, as "the righteous man from the east," Isaiah 41:2.

Note of Interests: Many scholars believe the prophet Daniel while in Babylonian captivity, influenced the Babylonian and Persian empires, which led to the Magi familiarity with the Jewish scriptures, especially, "the star, and the birth of the king of the Jews."

The 1st gift presented to Jesus by the Magi was a precious metal called gold. The other two gifts from the Magi were costly plant extracts, which were frankincense and myrrh. Scholars believe that these three gifts were chosen for spiritual symbolism about Jesus himself.

The Bible does not mention the significance of the gifts. However, scholars believe gold represents Jesus' earthy kingship and His deity. Frankincense symbolizes Jesus' priestly role, holiness, and His willingness to become a burnt offering. Myrrh symbolizes suffering, affliction, and Jesus' death.

Note of Interests: A Pharisee named Nicodemus, who was a member of the Sanhedrin, brought a mixture of myrrh and aloes, totaling about 75 pounds, to anoint Jesus' body, once removed from the cross on Calvary. Jews did not practice embalming, and the funeral spices were used to anoint the body and to help minimize unpleasant odors. In the Gospel of John, Nicodemus is mentioned 3 times, first in John 3:1 – 21, his visit with Jesus; then John 7:50 – 51, defending Jesus against his colleagues, and finally, in John 19:39 – 42, when he appeared after the crucifixion of Jesus and assisted Joseph of Arimathea in preparing the body of Jesus for burial.

Frankincense and myrrh have been produced over 5,000 years in East Africa and the Arabian Peninsula. Frankincense and myrrh were burned during the Babylonians and Assyrians' religious ceremonies. Myrrh, when burned, has a woodsy, earthy fragrant, and frankincense is described as having piney, fragrant combined with a sweet, woody smell.

The Egyptians brought boatloads of the frankincense and myrrh resins from the Phoenicians. The frankincense and myrrh were used in incense, perfume, ointments for sores and battle wounds, as well as an insect repellent.

The Egyptian women used myrrh oil as a facial treatment, while frankincense was charred and ground into a powder to make the heavy black eyeliners the Egyptian women wore.

In Jerusalem's temple, frankincense and myrrh were components of the holy incense. The Greeks and Romans also used massive amounts of frankincense and myrrh incense during cremations.

Myrrh and frankincense are both obtained from a tree by making incisions in the bark. Frankincense and myrrh are both used in cosmetics and perfumes. They are also used as an antiseptic and analgesic.

Myrrh's scientific name is Commiphora myrrha. Myrrh grows on a small, thorny shrub-like, which grows about 16 feet tall. Myrrh has thin, dry bark, scattered bunches of leaves growing in pairs, and flowers with white petals and a yellow or red center. Myrrh is a reddish resin, which is located within the bark. Once an incision is made into the bark, the sap slowly oozes from the cut, drips down the tree, and forms tear-shaped droplets that are left to harden on the side of the tree, and then collected after two weeks.

Myrrh has been known to be mingled with wine to form an article of drink for relieving pain. Such a drink was offered to Jesus by the Roman soldiers while He hung on the cross being crucified. Myrrh is also referred to as "gall," in the Bible, Matthew 27:34, Mark 15:23.

Note of Interests: Myrrh was used for the purification of Queen Esther, Esther 2:12.

———◆◆◆◆◆———

Boswellia sacra is the scientific name for frankincense. Frankincense is extracted and harvested, like myrrh. It is a milky white sap taken out of the Boswellia tree. The sap is collected by cutting an incision to the inner bark of the tree.

The sap slowly oozes out of the incision, and form into balls on the outside of the tree, which are collected and sold. The sap will eventually turn a light orangish-brown color. In July, bright, perky white and pink flowers will bloom on the tree.

Note of Interests: The Greek Historian Herodotus reported that the sap of the frankincense trees was dangerous to harvest because of the poisonous snakes that lived in the trees. The Arabians overcame the problem by burning the sap of myrrh and frankincense trees, which drove the snakes away. In the Egyptians, Greeks, and Romans folklores, frankincense was used for driving away evil spirits from the human body.

CHAPTER 13
HYSSOP

Hyssop is an herb in the mint family with cleansing, medicinal, therapeutic, and flavoring properties that was prolific in the Middle East. The dried hyssop is used as an herbal tea and used to flavor alcoholic beverages. Hyssop is an aromatic perennial plant, which is resistant to drought, grows in rocky soil, thrives in hot climates, pollinated by bees, and grows about 4 feet tall.

Scholars believe the Origanum syriacum to be the hyssop mentioned in the Bible. The Origanum syriacum is commonly called Syrian oregano or zaatar. It is also known as Majorana syriaca, bible hyssop, Biblical-hyssop, or Lebanese oregano.

The Origanum syriacum is native to the Mediterranean area. It is a semi-woody plant in the mint family called Lamiaceae or Labiatae. The mint family includes over 200 genera and 6,000 species, which are mostly herbaceous plants (non-woody plants), but some are shrubs and trees. The majority of the plants in the mint family are aromatic and widely used as culinary herbs like basil, bay leaf, parsley, rosemary, sage, savory, marjoram, oregano, thyme, lavender, mentha, dill, cilantro, along with hyssop.

The Origanum syriacum is harvested twice a year, at the end of spring, and the beginning of the fall. Hyssop flowers and leaves have been highly valued since ancient times. Hyssops are preferably harvested when they are blossoming, so the flowering buds can be collected. The spring growth shoots forth from the ground and rapidly grows.

The early growth of the Origanum syriacum has bright green leaves and reddish stems. The leaves are harvested at this stage until the bloom has been on the branch for a while. The hyssop's leaves have a slightly bitter, and an intense minty aroma. As the leaves age, they will become dark dusty green, and the stems will become woody brown. The old leaves can be dried and powdered.

In the winter, the flower buds will be elongated. The new flower buds can be used fresh or dried. The shrub can be cut back to the ground to rest for winter, or the small flowers, which are white, or pink can be left on the shrub for bees, wasps, and other insects.

The Bible mentions "hyssop" mostly in the Old Testament. Hyssop is mentioned 12 times in the Bible, 10 times in the Old Testament, and only twice in the New Testament. The word "hyssop" is mentioned 5 times in the Book of Leviticus, chapter 14. The Hebrew word for hyssop is "ezov," and hyssop is mentioned first in Exodus 12:22.

**And ye shall take a bunch of hyssop,
and dip it in the blood that is in the bason,
and strike the lintel and the two
side posts with the blood
that is in the bason;
and none of you shall go out at the door
of his house until the morning.**
Exodus 12:22 KJV

Hyssop was used by the Levitical priests extensively. At Passover, hyssop was used to sprinkle the blood of the sacrificial lamb on the doorposts of the Israelites' homes. Moses told the elders of Israel to tell the people to take a bunch of hyssop, dip it in the blood of the Passover lamb and put the blood on the doorposts for the angel of death to pass over their dwelling places, Exodus 12:22. God was going to perform His 10th plague against the Egyptians, which was the death of the 1st born when the Israelites were slaves in Egypt being abused, overworked, and punished by their slave masters.

According to Leviticus 14 and Numbers 19, hyssop was used for ritual cleansing. God commanded His people to use hyssop in the ceremonial cleansing of people and houses. The priests would use hyssop together with cedarwood, scarlet yard, and the blood of a clean bird, and sprinkle it over a person recently healed from a skin disease, like leprosy, rashes, or scabies. Once the priest performed this act, the person would now be ceremonially cleansed from the diseased, and allowed to reenter the camp, Leviticus 14:1 – 9. A similar ceremonial act was performed to purify a house that previously had mildew or mold, Leviticus 14:48 – 53.

According to 1 Kings 4:29 – 34, Solomon's wisdom was greater than the wisdom of all the people of the East, and the wisdom of Egypt. He spoke 3,000 proverbs, and his songs numbered 1,005. Solomon spoke about plant life, hyssop, beasts, animals, birds, creeping things, and fish.

And he (Solomon) spake of trees,
from the cedar tree that is in Lebanon
even unto the hyssop

that springeth out of the wall;
he spake also of beasts, and of fowl, and
of creeping things, and of fishes.
1 Kings 4:33 KJV

David mentioned hyssop in Psalm 51:7, and it reads, "Purge me with hyssop, and I shall be clean: wash me, and I shall be whiter than snow." According to scholars, David is not referring to physical cleansing; David is asking God to cleanse him spiritually as he confesses his sin.

In the Gospel of John, hyssop was presented at Jesus' crucifixion. The Roman soldiers offered Jesus a drink of wine vinegar on a sponge at the end of hyssop, and this is recorded as the last act that happened before Jesus declared His work on earth was finished and gave up His spirit, John 19:29 – 30.

According to Hebrews 9:19 – 20, after Moses had read every precept of God's commandments to the people, he used scarlet wool, and hyssop, and took the blood of calves and goats, with water, and sprinkled the book of God's law and all the people. Moses then told the people that the blood confirms the covenant God has made with the Israelites, and in the same manner, Moses sprinkled blood on the Tabernacle, and everything used for worship.

Note of Interests: Hyssop is used by beekeepers to produce a thicker, sweet-smelling, and flavorful honey.

CHAPTER 14

BARLEY AND WHEAT

Barley and wheat were two of the mainstays of the common people's diet in Bible days. Barley was eaten regularly and was a dominant portion of their diet. According to 1 Kings 4:28, barley was also used as fodder.

> **They also brought the necessary barley and straw for the royal horses in the stables.**
> 1 Kings 4:28 NLT

Barley was coarser than wheat and was not as tasty. Barley was the main food of the poor and became labeled the "poor man's bread." It has always been valued less than wheat. According to Revelation 6:6, a quart of wheat cost a whole day's wages, but for a whole day's wage for barley, 3 quarts of barley can be purchased.

Barley is planted around December, and the grain can be planted on soil without plowing. Barley can be grown in areas too dry for wheat. The barley grains mature at the end of April, or the beginning of May, about a month before wheat, Exodus 9:31 – 32.

In the sunlight, when the barley fields are ripened for harvest, they appear white, spoken by Jesus to his disciples in John 4:27 – 38.

> Say not ye, There are yet four months
> and then cometh harvest?
> Behold, I say unto you, lift up your
> eyes, and look on the fields;
> for they are white already to harvest.
> John 4:35 KJV

In appearance, barley has a longer tassel of plant hair protecting the kernels, which is called the beard, and wheat has a shorter beard. Before flowering, barley can be confused with other small grains. Barley is distinguished from wheat, rye, and oats by examining the leaf collar when it is pulled away from the stem. The leaf collar on a barley plant will have 2 overlapping appendages that connect firmly to the plant stem. Barley grows 2 – 4 feet tall, and the seeds are developed on a long stem with flower clusters in groups of 3 long bristles about 6 inches long. When the barley is ready for harvesting, it turns golden brown, and wheat will be slightly yellow.

Note of Interests: There are two different groups of barley, which are called the six-row, and the two-row. These groups refer to the difference in the configuration of the blooms attached to the stem. The 6 rows barley, the kernel size is smaller than the two-row barley.

Barley was widely cultivated and an important food crop for the people in Bible days, until the 16th century when farmers in the Middle East began to grow wheat for food. Barley is still an important crop surrounding Bethlehem, and there are still small plots of barley, which is harvested by hand, as described in the Book of Ruth. The women would cut the grain, then tie them into bundles to dry. When the barley is dried, it was taken by donkeys to the threshing floors, and there it was threshed using a threshing sledge pulled by an animal, Deuteronomy 25:4.

According to Leviticus 23:9 – 14, the Israelites were instructed to "bring the priest a bundle of grain from the first fruit of their grain harvest." In the Book of Ruth, Boaz was a successful and wealthy farmer who had a barley field. Boaz honors the LORD, and according to Ruth 2:2, when he harvested the field of barley, he left grain for the poor, in accordance with ordinances of the land, Leviticus 23:22.

Note of Interests: In some Bible translations, wheat and barley are referred to as corn. For example, Matthew 12:1 reads, "At that time Jesus went through the grainfields on the Sabbath. His disciples were hungry and began to pick some heads of grain and eat them," NIV. The KJV of Matthew 12:1 reads, "At that time Jesus went on the sabbath day through the corn; and his disciples were an hungred and began to pluck the ears of corn and to eat." The J. B. Philipps New Testament, Authorized King James Version, and Wycliffe Bible are other Bible translations that use the word "corn." In Great Britain, the word "corn" refers to small grain and includes barley, wheat, and rye.

<hr />

Barley is harvested first, around the time of Passover, and wheat is harvest next, around the time of Pentecost. Grapes are collected around the time of Sukkot.

Passover is the Jewish festival celebrating the exodus from Egypt and the Israelites' freedom from slavery to the Egyptians. Pentecost is generally called "the birthday of the Church" because, on this day, the descent of the Holy Spirit occurred. Sukkot is also called Tabernacles, Tents, or Booths, which honors the 40 years the Israelites spent in the desert, depending, and trusting only on God for their sustenance.

Passover, Pentecost, and Sukkot are the three main "Pilgrimage Festivals," in which the entire population of the kingdom of Judah made a pilgrimage to the Temple in Jerusalem, as commanded by the law of God. The distance between Judah and Jerusalem was approximately 87 miles.

Barley bread was multiplied in two biblical events in the Bible. A man from Baalshalishah brought barley bread and barley grain to Elisha to eat, but Elisha ordered that it be provided as food for the people, 2 Kings 4:42. After the people had eaten, there was much barley bread leftover. In John 6, Jesus feeds 5,000 people with 5 barley loaves and 2 small fishes, and afterward, everyone had eaten there were 12 baskets of barley bread leftover.

Note of Interests: According to Numbers 5:11 – 31, the "jealousy offering" is the only offering that specifically requires 2 quarts of barley flour for the ritual to be performed. It was an offering the husband brought to the priest when he charged his wife with adultery, being unfaithful. The husband would present his wife before the priest, and he would create a liquid mixture for the wife to drink. The mixture the priest made consisted of holy water placed in a clay jar and dust taken from the Tabernacle floor. This liquid mixture was called "the jar of bitter water." If the wife were guilty of adultery, she would get sick, and her belly would swell. If the wife were innocent, God would protect her from the effects of "the jar of bitter water." According to Leviticus 20:10, if a wife was found guilty of adultery, the punishment was death.

Barley is mentioned in 35 verses in the Bible, 32 times in the Old Testament and 3 times in the New Testament. Barley is mentioned first in the Book of Exodus, and the most in the Book of Ruth, a total of 6 times. Wheat is mentioned in 51 verses in the Bible, 39 times in the Old Testament, and 12 times in the New Testament. Wheat is mentioned first in Genesis 30:14, and the most in the books of Jeremiah and Matthew, 4 times each.

Wheat, like barley, rye, maize, and oats, is a cereal grain, and cereal grains are members of one of the largest families of grass flowering plants. Wheat is grown on more land area than any other food crop, more than 540,000,000 acres. Wheat is used for making flour, bread, pasta, pies, cakes, baskets, bedding, whereas barley is used as one of the primary ingredients used for the creation of alcoholic drinks. Barley is the component of various health foods, used in soups, stews, and bread.

Note of Interests: The chaff of wheat and barley were used in making traditional bricks, Exodus 5:6 – 23.

There are several species of wheat, and the wheat which Pharaoh saw in his dream was the Triticum compositum, which bears seven head of grain upon one single stalk, Genesis 41:5 – 7. Two other kinds of wheat grown in Israel were Triticum vulgare and the Triticum spelta. In the parable of the sower in Matthew 13:8, the LORD mentioned grains of wheat, which produces a hundred-fold in good ground. The Triticum vulgare is known to produce 100 grains in the ear of a single stalk. The ear is the grain-bearing tip part of the stem of a cereal plant, such as wheat or maize. The ears consist of stems on which tightly packed rows of flowers grow. Triticum vulgare is the most widely grown wheat crop produced, about 95%.

According to Deuteronomy 8:8, wheat and barley were two of the divine provisions God promised the Israelites in the "Promise Land."

**So, obey the commands of the LORD your God
by walking in his ways and fearing him.
For the LORD your God is bringing
you into a good land
of flowing streams and pools of water,
with fountains and springs
that gush out in the valleys and hills.
It is a land of wheat and barley; of grapevines, fig trees,
and pomegranates; of olive oil and honey.
It is a land where food is plentiful,
and nothing is lacking.**
Deuteronomy 8:6 – 8 NLT

CHAPTER 15
FLAX TO LINEN

Linum usitatissimum is the scientific name for flax. The word "usitatissimum" means "most useful." Usitatissimum seems to be a perfect name for a plant that is used for both food and clothing. Flax is grown for its fiber, seeds, and oil. When flax matures, they have sky-blue flowers that open only in the morning. It grows over 3 feet tall, with slender stems. Flax is considered one of the most beautiful of all crops when flowering and is often planted as an ornamental.

After flax is harvested, the plants are dried, and the seeds are removed through a process called threshing and winnowing. The seeds in the flax can be grounded into a meal and made into an oil, called flaxseed or linseed. Flax oil has a high level of protein, dietary fiber, B vitamins, and minerals. The oil is also used as a drying agent for paintings, and a varnished in products, such as linoleum.

Note of Interests: In the 10 verses in the Bible where flax is mentioned, the seeds are not mentioned being eating by the Israelites, Exodus 9:31, Joshua 2:6, Judges 15:14, Proverbs 31:13, Isaiah 19:9, Isaiah 42:3, Ezekiel 40:3, Hosea 2:5, Hosea 2:9, and Matthew 12:20.

Flaxseed is often used as feed for chickens, horses, and pigs. The flax straw that is left over from the harvested of the oilseeds is hard to digestible and is not generally used as animal feed for cattle, or sheep, but is used as bedding.

In biblical days, clothes for the people were made from fig leaves, animal skins, wool, silk, and flax. The Bible makes no mention of cotton as a clothing material used by the Israelites, but it was used in early times in the Middle East.

In the English Stand Version Bible (ESV), the word "cotton" is only mentioned twice in Esther 1:6, and Isaiah 19:9. However, in the same verse, the word "cotton" is not used in the KJV, NLT, and NIV. Scholars believe cotton was grown in Judea around 490 BC. It was discovered that some Egyptian child mummies were wrapped in cotton bandages. The Israelites learned about growing cotton, while they were in captivity in Persia under King Ahasuerus (KJV, WEB), 598 – 536 BC.

Note of Interests: King Ahasuerus' name is spelled Xerxes in the NIV and NLT Bible translations. Ahasuerus is the king's name in Hebrew, and Xerxes is his name in the Greek derivation.

However, much of all clothing in Bible days were made from either flax or wool. Flax comes from a plant fiber, and wool comes from shearing fleece from a living animal, especially a sheep.

Note of Interests: According to Genesis 4:2, Abel was called "a keeper of sheep." It is not known, if Abel raised sheep for their wool, the Bible does not say.

Flax was an essential plant because of its fibers and was cultivated during biblical times. The fibers are removed from the stalk, and the other parts, such as linseed, shives, and tows, are set aside for other uses. Flax shives are used as paper for some cigarettes, and in some plastic products. Flax tows are coarse broken fiber, removed while processing flax, and often used as upholstery stuffing.

Flax seeds are sown in the winter and flowers in late spring. The flax plant is harvested when it is nearly full-grown. The stalks can be dried in the sun; then afterward, they are soaked in water to soften the woody stalk parts because the fibers must be loosened from the stalks.

Note of Interests: Scholars believe this is why Rahab, the harlot, had bundles of flax on her roof, allowing them to dry, Joshua 2:6. In the United States, North Dakota grows much of the flax that is produced.

The stalks are beaten, and the fibers are separated, or sorted out, and spun into yarns of thread for weaving. The plant fibers are eventually woven into a fabric called linen, which is extremely strong, and absorbent. The fabric can then be bleached or dyed.

Note of Interests: To produce the longest possible flax fibers, the flax is either hand-harvested by pulling up the plant or cutting it close to the root.

<hr/>

Flax is only mentioned in 10 verses in the KJV, but the fabric that flax is woven into is mentioned in 90 verses. The word "linen" is mentioned in 74 verses in the Old Testament, and 16 verses in the New. The linen fabric in many of the verses in the Bible is described as "fine linen."

The earliest Biblical reference to "fine linen" is the garment that Pharaoh placed on Joseph in the 18th century, Genesis 41:42. Linen is described as "fine linen" in the KJV Bible 31 times.

> **And Pharaoh took off his ring from his hand,**
> **and put it upon Joseph's hand, and arrayed**
> **him in vestures of fine linen,**
> **and put a gold chain about his neck.**
> Genesis 41:42 KJV

According to Exodus 26:1, the tabernacle 10 curtains were made from "fine twined linen." The phrase "fine twined linen" is mentioned 20 times, and only in the Book of Exodus, in chapters 26, 27, 28, 36, 38, and 39.

According to Exodus 28 and 39, Israel's High Priest's garment under the Levitical Order was made from linen, and the priest is described as wearing a "linen ephod." A linen ephod was a garment worn outside the robe of the priest. The ephod was made of fine twined linen. The garment was blue, purple, and scarlet, with a gold embroidered thread, Exodus 28:4, Exodus 29:5, Exodus 39:2.

Angels also wore white linen in the New Testament, Revelation 15:6. The significance of linen, when worn as clothing represented personal holiness and implies that the individual clothed in linen is in a good moral-ethical standard with God, and can approach Him.

Note of Interests: Around 9 BC, the prophet Elijah could be recognized by a description of the clothing he wore. 2 Kings 1:8 NIV reads, "They replied, He had a garment of hair and a leather belt around his waist." The king said, "That was Elijah the Tishbite." Around the Spring of 26 AD, hundreds of years later, John the Baptist begins his public ministry, and people thought he was Elijah, perhaps because of the similarity of their clothing. Matthew 3:4 KJV reads, "And the same John had his raiment of camel's hair, and a leathern girdle about his loins; and his meat was locusts and wild honey."

<hr />

According to Ezekiel 40, fourteen years after the fall of Jerusalem, the LORD took Ezekiel in a vision to the land of Israel and set him on a high mountain. He could see a man whose face shone like bronze standing at the gateway of Jerusalem. The man was holding in his hand a flax linen measuring cord and a measuring rod. The LORD told Ezekiel about the new Temple that was to be built.

Note of Interests: The word "linen" is related to the word "line" because the fabric threads are woven in a straight line. The word "linen" also relates to other words, including lining, lingerie, linear, and lineage.

-------◆◆◆◆◆-------

Prehistoric caves in the Republic of Georgia located in the southeastern parts of Europe suggested the use of woven linen fabric from wild flax may date back over 30,000 years ago. In ancient Mesopotamia, flax was cultivated and made into linen, where the priests and wealthy mainly used and wore linen. In ancient Egypt, linen was used for burial wrappings, mummification. When the tomb of Pharaoh Ramses II, was discovered in 1881, the linen wrappings were in excellent condition and had preserved the body well, after more than 3,000 years.

Note of Interests: According to Deuteronomy 22:11, Leviticus 19:19, in Judaism, it was prohibited by law to wear clothing made of wool and linen, along with planting your field with 2 different kinds of seeds or mating 2 different types of animals.

-------◆◆◆◆◆-------

In Proverbs 31, the word "linen" is used to describe a noble wife.

She makes her own bedspreads.
She dresses in fine linen and purple gowns.
Proverbs 31:22 NLT

Note of Interests: In the United States, cotton is used instead of linen because linen costs more to manufacture than cotton. In the past, linen was used for making book covers due to its strength. Linen was used in cooking to hold dough in place, while it rises to its final shape. Linen was one of the preferred underlying support for oil paintings, and due to its strength in the Middle Ages, linen was used to make shields, bowstrings, and body armors. The United States' currency paper is made from 25% linen and 75% cotton.

According to John 19:40, after Jesus' death, his body was wrapped in linen cloths.

**So they took Jesus' body,
and bound it in linen cloths with the spices,
as the custom of the Jews is to bury.**
John 19:40 WEB

Question: Who is "they" referring to in John 19:40 verse? smile

The answer is in the back of the book

1. _____

2. _____

CHAPTER 16
BULRUSHES

According to Exodus 2, Moses' birth mother was named Jochebed. She placed her 3-month-old son in a basket, she made from bulrushes and waterproofed it with tar and pitch. Around 1392 BC, when Jochebed's son was born, Pharaoh issued a decree to kill all the Hebrew's baby boys because they were becoming so numerous and begun to outnumber the Egyptians. Pharaoh feared once they became young men, they would revolt against their Egyptian slave masters and Egypt.

Jochebed placed the infant child in the basket in the reeds on the bank of the Nile River to avoid detection by the Egyptian authorities. She then set him adrift on the Nile River in what is described in KJV as an "ark of bulrushes," Exodus 2:3. The "ark of bulrushes" was a floating carrier that resembles a basket, cradle, or tiny boat. Jochebed had Moses' sister, Miriam, to watch the basket as it drifts along the Nile riverbank.

Note of Interests: Now, the "ark of bulrushes" plant is widely cultivated as an ornamental plant, which is also called "Moses-in-the-cradle." It is described as a plant with long shaped leaves, and the flower in the center of the leaves appear to be in an enclosure that looks like a baby bassinet.

Pharaoh's daughter came out to bathe in the Nile River with her attendants. Scholars believe her name was Bithiah. The princess saw the bulrush basket at the edge of the riverbank; she sent one of her attendants to get it for her. When the princess opened the basket, she saw the baby crying and said, "this must be one of the Hebrew children."

Miriam was watching out of sight at a distance and observed what had happened. She quickly approached the princess and asked should she go and find one of the Hebrew women to nurse the baby for her, and the princess said, "yes." Miriam went and got the baby's mother, and she nursed him, and the princess did not know it was the child's mother. Pharaoh's daughter raised the infant as her son, and she named the infant, Moses, because she said, "I lifted him out of the water."

Note of Interests: The Ancient Egyptians built boats from bulrush plants that grew along the Nile River in Egypt. The Nile River is approximately 4,135 miles long, located in northeastern Africa, and the longest in the world. Bulrush boats are still used in Peru, Bolivia, and Ethiopia, as fishing boats, and for hunting seabirds. The prophet Isaiah refers to Ethiopian vessels of bulrushes upon the water in Isaiah 18:2.

The word "bulrush" is a common name for large wetland, grassy-like plants in the sedge plant family called Cyperaceae. The sedge family has around 5,500 known species, described in approximately 90 genera. Scholars believe the Cyperus papyrus is the plant, which is mentioned in the Biblical event of baby Moses being placed in the "ark of bulrushes" by his mother.

The Cyperus papyrus is an herbaceous perennial aquatic flowering plant in the sedge family, Cyperaceae. The Cyperus papyrus is commonly called papyrus. Once these plants are established, they grow extremely fast, and if their roots are sunken in water or very moist soil, the plant will blossom all year long. The tall aquatic plants are known to grow up to 16 feet tall, and between 2 - 5 feet wide. A dense flowering head tops each of the triangle's stems called the umbel that sprouts from the woody rhizomes.

When the new plant shoot grows, the umbel remains closed until its stem has grown above its other plants that have blossomed, then it opens to reveal a large bright green, thin, ray-like spikes that may bear tiny flowers, which grows about 10 inches long, and resemble a feather duster when the plant is young. The flower clusters will eventually give way to brown, nut-like fruits.

Note of Interests: Schoenoplectus, Bolboschoenus, and Cyperus are recognized as having edible seeds. Bulrush seeds are generally consumed by ducks, wild geese, birds, and muskrats.

The beautiful Cyperus papyrus plant and its close relatives have an exceptionally long history with civilization. Throughout the hot climates of Africa and in the Mediterranean countries, the papyrus flourishes abundantly, near perimeters, like ponds, marshes, lakes, rivers, and flooded swamps.

Note of Interests: The Cyperus papyrus is near extinction in its native environment, the Nile Delta. Remember, a delta is where silt and sediments accumulate at the mouth of a large river, and most of Egypt's habitable land is within the Nile Delta and along the Nile River.

In Egypt between 2686 – 2181 BC, papyrus stems were used in religious ceremonies. Papyrus stems were presented to Hathor, the goddess of love and joy. In the search for a favor from gods, papyrus scepters were given to them. To show respect to the gods, the people would weave papyrus flowering heads into a wreath and presented it to them. Papyrus designs were discovered in the scenery of wall painting in kings' tombs. Ancient Egyptians used papyrus as a source of paper, which was one of the first types of paper created. Scholars state that the earlier versions of the Bible were recorded on Papyrus paper.

Young papyrus shoots can be eaten cooked or raw. The papyrus woody root was made into bowls, food utensils, and burned for fuel. From the papyrus stems, reed boats, boat sails, floor mats, cloth, and sandals are made. In the Okavango Delta, the fishermen use small sections of the plant stems as floats for their nets. The feather-duster flowering heads make a nesting site for many types of birds.

Note of Interests: In 1969 and 1970, the famous explorer Thor Heyerdahl built two reed boats from papyrus to demonstrate that ancient African or Mediterranean people could have made long sea voyages. The most notable expedition was in 1970 on the boat named Ra II. Heyerdahl sailed with a diverse crew from the west coast of Africa to Barbados, approximately 5,307 miles. The boat named Ra II is now in the Kon-Tiki Museum in Oslo, Norway. A book about the voyage is written titled, <u>The Ra Expeditions,</u> and a film documentary was made about the voyage, also.

In some Bible translations, the word "bulrushes" is referred to as "papyrus." The KJV Bible does not use the word "papyrus," but "bulrushes." The word "bulrushes" is only mentioned twice in the KJV Bible, in Exodus 2 and Isaiah 18.

King James Version (KJV), Bulrushes is mentioned in 2 verses:

Exodus 2:3, And when she could not longer hide him, she took for him an ark of **bulrushes**, and daubed it with slime and with pitch, and put the child therein; and she laid it in the flags by the river's bank.

Isaiah 18:1 – 2, Woe to the land shadowing with wings, which is beyond the rivers of Ethiopia: 2) That sendeth ambassadors by the sea, even in vessels of **bulrushes** upon the waters, saying, Go, ye swift messengers, to a nation scattered and peeled, to a people terrible from their beginning hitherto; a nation meted out and trodden down, whose land the rivers have spoiled!

The Bible translation, in which verses are used for this book, are KJV, NIV, NLT, and WEB. The word "papyrus" was mentioned in NIV, NLT, and WEB, but not necessarily in all the same verses as the KJV or the other translations. It's very interesting, so those verses have been recorded below. However, papyrus is only mentioned in the Old Testament in each Bible translation.

New International Version (NIV), Papyrus is mentioned in 5 verses:

Exodus 2:3, But when she could hide him no longer, she got a **papyrus** basket for him and coated it with tar and pitch. Then she placed the child in it and put it among the reeds along the bank of the Nile.

Job 8:11, Can **papyrus** grow tall where there is no marsh? Can reeds thrive without water?

Job 9:26, They skim past like boats of **papyrus**, like eagles swooping down on their prey.

Isaiah 18:1 – 2, Woe to the land of whirring wings, along the rivers of Cush, 2) which sends envoys by sea in **papyrus** boats over the water. Go, swift messengers, to a people tall and smooth-skinned, to a people feared far and wide, an aggressive nation of strange speech, whose land is divided by rivers.

Isaiah 35:7, The burning sand will become a pool, the thirsty ground bubbling springs. In the haunts where jackals once lay, grass and reeds and **papyrus** will grow.

New Living Translation (NLT), Papyrus is mentioned in 3 verses:

Exodus 2:3, But when she could no longer hide him, she got a basket made of **papyrus** reeds and waterproofed it with tar and pitch. She put the baby in the basket and laid it among the reeds along the bank of the Nile River.

Job 8:11, Can **papyrus** reeds grow tall without a marsh? Can marsh grass flourish without water?

Job 9:26, It disappears like a swift **papyrus** boat, like an eagle swooping down on its prey.

Isaiah 18:1 – 2, Listen, Ethiopia land of fluttering sails that lies at the headwaters of the Nile, 2) that sends ambassadors in <u>swift</u> boats down the river. Go, swift messengers! Take a message to a tall, smooth-skinned people, who are feared far and wide for their conquests and destruction, and whose land is divided by rivers.

Note: Isaiah 18:2 NLT describes the boats as "swift" and not as "papyrus boats" like the NIV, and WEB translations.

World English Bible (WEB), Papyrus is mentioned in 3 verses:

Exodus 2:3, When she could no longer hide him, she took a **papyrus** basket for him, and coated it with tar and with pitch. She put the child in it and laid it in the reeds by the river's bank.

Job 8:11, Can the **papyrus** grow up without mire? Can the rushes grow without water?

Isaiah 18:1 – 2, Ah, the land of the rustling of wings, which is beyond the rivers of Ethiopia; 2) that sends ambassadors by the sea, even in vessels of **papyrus** on the waters, saying, "Go, you swift messengers, to a nation tall and smooth, to a people awesome from their beginning onward, a nation that measures out and treads down, whose land the rivers divide!"

CHAPTER 17
ALTAR OF INCENSE

The phrase "altar of incense" is mentioned 6 times in the KJV. The "altar of incense" is mentioned first in Exodus 30 as one of the items inside the Holy Place of the Tabernacle. When the priests enter the Holy Place, they would see the table of showbread on the right, a golden lampstand on the left, and the altar of incense was straight ahead.

The Holy Place was 30 feet long, 15 feet wide, and 15 feet high. The front of the tabernacle tent had a veil made of blue, purple, and scarlet yarn hung from 4 golden pillars. The altar of incense was made from acacia wood, overlaid with pure gold. The height of the "altar of incense" was 21 inches high and 21 inches wide. The top of the altar was square with a horn at each corner.

Four rings of gold were built on the altar of incense so that acacia poles could be slipped through the rings to carry the altar. The "altar of incense" was located in front of the veil that separated the Holy Place from the Holy of Holies, and the "ark of the covenant" was located on the other side of the veil; this is where the presence of God appeared.

Aaron was instructed to burn fragrant incense on the altar each morning and at twilight, as a regular offering to the LORD. God gave the ingredients for making the incense and commanded that no other incense should ever be burned on the altar.

Note of Interests: Throughout the Bible, incense is associated with prayer. According to Psalm 141:2, David prayed, "May my prayer be set before you like incense." According to Revelation 5:8, in John's vision of heaven, he saw the elders around the throne. The elders were holding golden bowls full of incense, which were the prayers of God's people. According to Luke 1:10, when Zechariah, the priest, was offering incense in the temple, a great number of people were standing outside the temple praying, at the hour of incense.

According to Exodus 30, the sacred incense used in the Tabernacle was made from the flowering plants, stacte (gum resin), onycha, galbanum, and pure frankincense.

> **And the LORD said unto Moses,**
> **Take unto thee sweet spices, stacte,**
> **and onycha, and galbanum;**
> **these sweet spices with pure frankincense:**
> **of each shall there be a like weight:**
> Exodus 30:34 – 36 KJV

The Israelites and the generations to come were to burn incense before the LORD, Exodus 30:7 – 9. The incense was burned on the "altar of incense" to thank and praise God for his protection to his redeemed people.

Stacte is the first ingredient mentioned in preparing the sacred incense. Stacte comes from the plant Styrax officinalis. In Israel, Styrax officinalis is called by several names, which are Official storax, stacte tree, and styrax. In

Israel, the styrax tree grows on the Judean and Samarian mountains. Some of the trees are located on Mount Carmel and Herman.

The Hebrew word for "stacte" is "nataph," which means to ooze or gradually come out in drops. In the NIV, New International Version Bible, stacte is translated as gum resin, Exodus 30:34.

> **Then the LORD said to Moses,**
> **"Take fragrant spices – gum resin,**
> **onycha, and galbanum**
> **– and pure frankincense, all in equal amounts,**
> **and make a fragrant blend of incense,**
> **the work of a perfumer.**
> **It is to be salted and pure and sacred."**
> Exodus 30:34 - 35 NIV

Styrax is classified as a tree, which can grow up to 52 feet in height. The Styrax officinalis exist in dry, rocky slopes, woods, thickets, and besides streams.

The stacte plant sheds its leaves, and in autumn, the leaves turn yellow and drop off the branches, and in spring, new leaves will sprout. In Israel, the styrax tree blooms in April through June. The tree will be covered with flowers that look like snowdrops. A highly aromatic resin is discharged when the styrax tree stems and branches are cut. The resin has been described as a sweet, earthly, smelling fragrance.

According to Exodus 30:34, onycha is the 2nd ingredient mentioned in the making of the sacred incense. It is the most controversial ingredient used in the sacred incense. The

Bible does not give any indication as to what onycha is; some Bible scholars believed that onycha came from a whelk-like shellfish that was common to the Red Sea area. Other scholars believe that onycha, which was also called rockrose bush or labdanum, is the ingredient in the incense. Still, others believe tragacanth, the gum resin from the astragalus plant species, is the ingredient.

Note of Interests: In ancient Egypt, labdanum resin from the rockrose bush stuck to the beard of goats that rambled in the rocks, where it grew. Labdanum was a grayish-black resin that was released from the branches of the rockrose.

Galbanum is the 3rd plant ingredient in the incense. The scientific name for galbanum is Ferula gummosa, and it is a member of the same family of carrots and parsley. The Hebrew word for galbanum is "chelb-nah." The only place that chelb-nah" appears in the Bible is with spices used to make the Tabernacle incense.

In England and the United States, the flowers were described as greenish-white or yellow. In Central Asia, the flowers are described as a dazzling orange-yellow in color. There are differing opinions about the resin odor, from a pleasant fragrant to a sharp, strong amora. Whatever was the scent of the galbanum plant alone, when it was blended with the other three spices, the resulting Tabernacle incense was a sweet, pleasing fragrance to God.

Frankincense is the 4th ingredient in the sacred incense, and was one of the gifts, the Wisemen brought the baby Jesus.

Frankincense fragrance is described as an aromatic piney scent.

The scientific name for frankincense is Boswellia sacra. Frankincense is a milky white sap taken from the Boswellia tree. The sap is collected by cutting an incision to the inner bark of the tree. The sap slowly oozes out of the incision, and form into balls on the outside of the tree. The sap will eventually turn a light orangish-brown color. In July, bright, perky white and pink flowers will bloom on the tree.

Note of Interests: In ancient civilization, the women used frankincense as part of a daily beauty routine. When frankincense is breathed in, it promotes a feeling of peace, satisfaction, and an overall sense of mental wellness.

CHAPTER 18

THE PRODIGAL SON

**The young man became so hungry
that even the pods he was feeding
the pigs looked good to him.
But no one gave him anything.**
Luke 15:16 NLT

According to Luke 15:11 – 32, Jesus spoke a parable of a lost son. In the parable, a man had two sons, and the younger son wanted his share of his father's estate. The father agreed to divide his wealth between his sons. A few days later, the younger son packed his belongings and moved to a far country, and there he squandered his estate with wild and foolish living.

After the prodigal son had spent all he had, he started working for a local farmer in that country, feeding pigs. According to verse 16 in Luke 15, the young man was so hungry that he longed to fill his stomach with the pods that the pigs ate.

According to scholars, the pods which the young man desired to eat were from the "Carob plant." The scientific name for "Carob" is "Ceratonia siliquar," and it is a flowering evergreen tree or shrub in the pea family.

Note of Interests: A botanist is an individual or individuals who studies plants and their various features and characteristics. The main difference between a tree and shrub is that a shrub has several main stems growing from the ground level, and a tree has one stem growing from the ground level called a trunk. Trees are also viewed as being over 20 feet tall, but not necessarily.

The carob plant is a native to Israel and grows up to 15 feet. The carob's name is not mentioned directly in the Bible, but scholars believe the pods may have been used as pig food, tempting the Prodigal son in Jesus' parable to fill his empty stomach.

The carob trees have a thick trunk with rough brown bark with sturdy branches. On the branches grows the long, curvy seedpods with a wrinkled surface that turns dark brown when it ripens. The carob's seedpod contains 5 to 18 hard brown seeds embedded in a sweet, thick, pulpy substance. It takes carob a year to develop, and once ripen, they drop to the ground.

The unripe carob pods are bright green, soft, and plump that looks very much like a pea pod. When the carob pods are ripened and dried, they can be toasted. Carob pods are naturally sweet and are often ground into carob powder. The carob shrub flowers are small and numerous. The red flowers blossom in spring, which is followed by long brown bean-like pods.

Note of Interests: The seeds of the carobs are the same size, and therefore, were used as a weight in eastern Mediterranean countries. The word "carat" comes from "carob." Nowadays, carobs are planted as ornamental shrubs or trees in gardens and landscapes.

<hr />

According to the remainder of the parable, the prodigal son came to his senses and decided to return home to his father. He decided he would confess his sins to his father and God. Then he would ask his father could he become a hired servant because he was no longer worthy of being called his son.

As the prodigal son was returning home, his father saw him from a long way off. His father ran to him, embraced him, and then kissed him. The father told his servant to bring his son the best robe quickly. The father placed a ring on his son's finger and sandals on his feet. The father had the fattest calf killed and held a celebration for his son because he was dead in sin and is alive again.

The older son had been working in the hot, dusty field; when he returned home, he heard music and dancing in the house. He asked a servant what all the commotion is about. The servant told him his brother had returned home, and his father was having a celebration.

The older son immediately became angry and refused to go in the house. So, the father came outside and pleaded with him. The older son told his father he had worked faithfully for him for years and always obeyed him, but he had never given him even a little goat so that he could have dinner with his friends.

The older son goes on to say to his father that the younger son left and wasted his money on prostitutes. Now, when he comes home, you ordered the best calf to be killed for a feast for him. The father replied, my son, you are always with me, and everything I have is yours, but we should be glad and celebrate because your brother was dead, but he is now alive; he was lost and has now been found, Luke 15:31 - 32.

CHAPTER 19
SEVEN FRESH BOWSTRINGS

**Samson answered her,
"If anyone ties me with seven fresh
bowstrings that have not been dried,
I'll become as weak as any other man."**
Judges 16:7 NIV

Samson was a judge from the tribe of Dan, and the last judge of the ancient Israelites. The birth and life of Samson are recorded in Judges 13 – 16. Samson was raised up by God to deliver the Israelites from the Philistines. God granted Samson supernatural strength, which he used to fight the Philistines who were occupying the Promised Land.

As Samson grew into a young man, he was attracted to non-Israelite women. Samson eventually fell in love with Delilah, who betrayed him to the 5 Lords of the Philistines, which ruled the territories of Ashkelon, Ashdod, Ekron, Gath, and Gaza. The Philistines were ancient people who lived on the south coast of the Promised Land, between the 12th century BC and 604 BC before they were exiled to Mesopotamia by King Nebuchadnezzar around 604 BC.

Note of Interests: The Bible mentions three Gentile women in Samson's life. The woman from Timnah was the first Gentile, non-Israelite woman Samson was involved with, and he married her. The second Gentile woman was the whore from Gaza, and the third was the only woman mentioned by name Delilah, with whom Samson fell in love with.

Beginning in Judges 13, God sent the Angel of the LORD to announce Samson's birth to his parents. Samson's father was named Manoah, but the name of Samson's mother is not given. The angel told them that Samson would be a Nazirite of God from the womb of his mother until the day of his death. A Nazirite was consecrated to God for service. According to Number 6, a Nazirite was to abstain from wine or strong drink, cannot drink grape juice or eat grapes or raisins, must keep his head unshaved, and stay away from dead bodies, Numbers 6:3 – 6.

Question: Who were the other two Nazirites for life? *Smile* . . .

1. _____
2. _____

The answer is in the back of the book

Note of Interests: The Philistines had oppressed Israelites 40 years, at the time of Samson's birth.

According to Judges 16, Samson fell in love with a beautiful woman in the Valley of Sorek, named Delilah. The Lords of the Philistines went to Delilah and asked her to find out where Samson's supernatural strength comes from, so they could capture him. The 5 Philistine Lords agreed to paid Delilah 1,100 shekels of silver each. Scholars are not sure about the value of the sum, but some scholars believe in today's currency; she was paid approximately $89,600 to betray Samson; other scholars believe it is much less.

Note of Interests: According to Judges 17:10, ten shekels of silver was a decent year's wage for a hired priest. Therefore, 1,100 shekels would have been 110 years' worth of pay. According to Jeremiah 32:9, Jeremiah paid 17 shekels for a field. In Zechariah, chapter 11, God told the prophet, Zechariah, to throw 30 silver pieces to the Potter in the Temple, and nearly 600 years later, Judas' 30 silver pieces bought the Potter's field, Matthew 27:9 – 10. According to Genesis 37, Joseph's brothers sold him into slavery for 20 pieces of silver.

Samson gave Delilah several answers about his strength and how to make him weak before he eventually told her the truth, and they are listed below.

First Answer, Judges 16:7 NIV

Samson answered her, "If anyone ties me with seven fresh bowstrings that have not been dried, I'll become as weak as any other man."

Second Answer, Judges 16:11 NIV

He said, "If anyone ties me securely with new ropes that have never been used, I'll become as weak as any other man."

Third Answer, Judges 16:13 NIV

Delilah then said to Samson, "All this time, you have been making a fool of me and lying to me. Tell me how you can be tied." He replied, "If you weave the seven braids of my head into the fabric on the loom and tighten it with the pin, I'll become as weak as any other man."

Samson became weary of Delilah's pleas for him to tell her the real source of his strength. Samson's revealed that his strength lay in his hair. When Samson fell asleep, Delilah called for someone to shave off the seven braids of Samson's hair. The Philistines seized Samson, gouged out his eyes, bound him in bronze shackles, and sent him down to Gaza to grind grain in prison.

According to Judges 16:22, the hair on Samson's head begins to grow back, and Samson repented for what he had done. The Philistines assembled in the temple to celebrate the delivery of Samson into their hands, and they brought Samson to the Dagon's temple to exhibit him to the crowds.

Samson asked the servant who accompanied him to the temple to place him between the two main temple pillars. There Samson prayed to God for the return of his strength, and God heard Samson prayer and gave him back his supernatural strength. Samson destroyed the Dagon temple and killed the people by pushing the main temple pillars down. On that day, Samson killed more than 3,000 Philistines; he killed more Philistines when he died than while he was living, Judges 16:30.

The first answer Samson gave Delilah concerning his supernatural strength was not true. Remember, Samson told Delilah, if anyone tied him with seven fresh bowstrings that have not been dried, he would become as weak as any other man. Bible researchers believed that the bowstrings, also known as throngs or ropes that Samson told Delilah, would make him weak as any other man was made from the Thymelaea hirsute plant, known in Hebrew as yitran.

According to Judges 16, the Philistines brought Delilah seven bowstrings, and Delilah tied Samson with them while the Philistines hid in a nearby chamber. Suddenly, Delilah called to Samson, "The Philistines are upon you." Samson snapped the yitran bowstrings with no hesitation and was victorious over his attackers.

The Thymelaea hirsute is known as yitran to Hebrews and as mitran to Arabs. Yitran is a perennial, evergreen shrub that grows abundantly in the Mediterranean coastal plain and the Sinai Peninsula. The yitran remains green throughout the year, even in the desert, because its roots grow extremely deep in the earth. The yitran is known to grow as tall as 6 feet in a well-water area. The yitran's stems are densely packed on the branches, and the arrangement of the branches gives the yitran shrub a bow shape. When the yitran branches are rubbed, or when the bark is peeled to make ropes, the yitran shrub gives off a sulfur-like odor.

Yitran branches were braided into thick ropes and cords and are strong enough to pull an animal out of a well. The

Philistines would have been aware of the strength of the seven braided thongs of yitran. Researchers believe that is why the Philistines believed that binding Samson with freshly braided yitran was the way to overpower his strength.

CHAPTER 20

CASTOR OIL PLANT

**And the LORD God provided a gourd,
and made it to come up over Jonah, that
it might be a shadow over his head,
to deliver him from his grief.
So Jonah was exceeding glad of the gourd.
But God prepared a worm when the
morning rose the next day,
and it smote the gourd that it withered.**
Jonah 4:6 – 7 KJV

Scholars believe that the "gourd" that gave Jonah shade was a castor oil shrub. The castor oil shrub is also known by other names like castor bean, gourd, and Palma Christi. The word "gourd" is mentioned 5 times in 4 verses in the KJV, Old Testament only, regarding the biblical event surrounding Jonah.

The word "gourd" with the "s" is mentioned once in 2 Kings 4:39, described as "wild gourds" that were poisonous. One of the servants placed wild gourds in a large pot and cooked it as a stew for the prophets. One of the prophets cried out that there is death in the pot! Elisha, the prophet, took some flour and made the poisonous stew, nonpoisonous, 2 Kings 4:38 – 41.

**And one went out into the field to gather herbs,
and found a wild vine, and gathered
thereof wild gourds his lap full,**

> **and came and shred them into the pot of**
> **pottage: for they knew them not.**
> 2 Kings 4:39 KJV

The scientific name for the castor oil shrub is Ricinus communis. The word "Ricinus" is a Latin word for the word "tick," and the word "communis" is Latin for the word "common." The castor oil seeds resemble the body of a tick, and that is why the name "Ricinus," was given to the plant by the botanist Carl Linnaeus, known as the "Father of Modern Taxonomy." Also, the castor oil seed is often called a bean, but it is not a bean. The castor oil plant is the only member of the genus Ricinus and is a native to Africa.

Throughout the Middle Ages, the castor oil plant was called "Palma Christi," which means "hand of Christ" because the leaf looks like a hand. The woody shrub grows about 16 feet high. The flowers appear in clusters, and on the Palma Christi stem, the male flowers grow at the base of the stem, producing white blossom. The female flowers are at the tip of the stem, and it produces pink round flowers that blossoms from March to November.

The castor oil plant has no petals, but 3 – 5 greenish sepals and numerous stamens. The sepal is the outer green leaf-like parts of the flower that develops around the flower bud. The long slender stalk and the pollen-producing anther is the male reproductive part of the flower called the stamen.

Shortly after the male flower reaches maturity, it will shed its pollen and die. In contrast, the female flowers develop the round capsule blossom. The blossom measure about ¾ in diameter and is covered with green or red flower buds that have sticky, stiff ends. When the female blossom capsule opens at maturity, it will reveal 3 smooth seeds that vary in color with grayish-brown specks. It is the seeds of the castor oil plants that have been of interest to civilization, and approximately 50% of the weight of the seeds is made of castor oil.

Castor oil has been used in the manufacturer of soaps, lubricants, hydraulic, and brake fluids, just to name a few. Castor oil is also used in medicine and perfumes.

Castor oil seeds have been found in Egyptian tombs dating back to 4000 BC.

Herodotus, the Greek historian, lived from 484 BC to 425 BC, noted the use of castor oil seeds for burning lamps, body ointment, to grow hair, and a laxative.

Note of Interests: In 1899, the Wakefield Oil Company was founded by Charles Cheers Wakefield. The company named was changed to "Castrol" around 1909 when researchers added castor oil to the company lubricant formulations, producing a new automotive lubricant that revolutionized transport in the first half of the 20th century. The company named "Castrol" is the contraction of "castor oil."

PS: Why don't you take a few minutes to refresh your memory concerning the Biblical event of Jonah, the big fish, Nineveh, the gourd, and the LORD's compassion? Let us read the Book of Jonah. Afterward, jot down what the LORD placed in your spirit concerning this biblical event. The Book of Jonah only has 4 short chapters that are outlined below.

Chapter 1 has 17 verses

1. Jonah Runs from the LORD
2. The Great Storm
3. Jonah Thrown in the Sea
4. Jonah Swallow by a Big Fish

Chapter 2 has 10 verses

1. The Prayer of Jonah
2. The LORD Spoke to the Fish

Chapter 3 has 10 verses

1. Jonah Goes to Nineveh and Preached
2. The King of Nineveh, People, and Animals Fasted

Chapter 4 has 11 verses

1. Jonah's Anger at the LORD's Compassion for Nineveh
2. The LORD Gourd for Jonah's Head
   Be Bless . . . In Jesus' Precious Name

CHAPTER 21
BIBLICAL EVENTS SURROUNDING PLANTS

Red Bud Tree

The Red Bud Tree is known as Judas' tree. According to Matthew 27:5, after Judas betrayed Jesus, he hanged himself. The Bible does not identify the tree Judas hung himself from, but the Red Bud Tree is believed by tradition to be the tree. Folklore states as Judas hung on the tree, the tree's white flowers turned red because the tree was ashamed that the betrayer of Jesus Christ died on it.

The biblical event of Judas' betrayal of Christ and suicide is recorded in Matthew 26 and 27. Judas was one of Jesus' original 12 disciples and the only non-Galilean apostle. He kept the money bag for Jesus and his followers. Judas objected to Mary anointing Jesus' feet with nard. Afterward, Judas went to the chief priests to negotiate money to betray Jesus, which was 30 silver coins, about 4 month's wages for a Jewish laborer, and the price of a slave in biblical days.

Tamarisk Tree

Some scholars believe that Hagar placed her son under a Tamarisk Tree in Genesis 21:15. She placed her son under the tree after their drinking water ran out. The Bible does not identify what type of tree Hagar put her son under, and therefore other scholars believe the tree could have been a Broom Tree.

According to Genesis 21:33 NIV, Abraham planted a Tamarisk Tree in Beersheba and worshipped the LORD. According to 1 Samuel 22:6, Saul sat under a tamarisk tree on the hill of Gibeah with his officials standing at his side. According to 1 Samuel 31:13 and 1 Chronicles 10:12, when the Philistines killed Saul and his sons, the people of Jabesh Gilead took down their bodies from the wall of Beth Shan and buried them under a Tamarisk Tree at Jabesh, and fasted 7 days. KJV Bible does not identify the type of tree; it just states "tree."

The Tamarisk Tree is common in and around Beersheba, and they can reach heights over 50 feet high. The tamarisk tree is an evergreen that has attractive pink or white flowers during the winter.

Abraham's Bush

One Jewish tradition teaches that the bush in which the ram was caught in was the Vitex agnus-castus. The Latin name Vitex agnus-castus refers to the life of the innocent lamb. The word "Vitex" means "life," "agnus" means "lamb," and "castus" means "humble."

According to Genesis 22, Abraham was commanded by the LORD to sacrifice his son Isaac. Abraham was being tested by the LORD to see if he would be obedient. The angel stopped Abraham from harming Isaac. According to Genesis 22:13, "Abraham looked and saw a ram caught in the thicket by his horns. He took the ram and offered him up as a sacrifice in place of his son."

Abraham's bush is also called the blackberry bush. The blackberry bush is a prickly scrambling shrub, and the plant produces long, thin branches that can reach 5 feet in length. The branches have spiked thorns that bend downward. When an individual reaches into the bush to pick fruit, they do not feel thorns, until they attempt to withdraw their hand. Initially, the blackberries are green, and as the fruit ripens, they turn red, then black.

Moses' Burning Bush

Scholars believe the Euonymus alatus is the burning bush Moses saw. Moses fled to Midian after killing an Egyptian. In Midian, Moses married Zipporah and became a shepherd for his father-in-law. One day, Moses led the flock to the backside of the desert and arrived at Mount Horeb. Moses noticed a bush was on fire, but the bush was not consumed by the fire. Moses decided to walk toward the burning bush to get a better view. Suddenly, God spoke from the bush; He told Moses to come no closer, he was standing on holy ground and take off his sandals. God told Moses that the Israelites were suffering under the slave masters in Egypt, and He was sending him to deliver and bring His people out of Egypt, Exodus 3:10.

Euonymus alatus is known as the "burning bush;" it is a large, spreading, deciduous shrub. In late spring to early summer, a wealth of tiny, greenish flowers appears before being replaced with purplish-red fruits that mature during the fall. The oval green leaves turn scarlet red in the fall before dropping to the ground.

Aloe

Aloe was popular for many reasons. It was used to cure, treat, and prevent diseases. Aloe was also used in Jewish burial customs and embalming the dead in Egypt. According to John 19:39 – 40, after Jesus died on the cross, Nicodemus brought a mixture of myrrh and aloes to prepare Jesus for burial. Nicodemus, with Joseph of Arimathea, wrapped Jesus' body with these spices, in strips of linen, verse 40.

The scientific name for Aloe is Aloe vera, and there are over 500 flowering species. Aloes ranges from small plants that are only a few inches in height to tall trees. Aloe blossoms in a cone shape with tubular flowers in the bright colors of red, orange, and yellow.

According to "A Love Song," Psalm 45, the king's robe was perfumed with myrrh, aloe, and cassia, while the music of string instruments made him glad in the ivory palace, verse 8.

Myrrh

The scientific name for myrrh is Commiphora myrrha. Myrrh was the most precious and expensive resin mentioned in the Bible. Myrrh is mentioned 16 times in the KJV, only 3 times in the New Testament. It was one of the gifts that the Magi brought to the newborn king, Matthew 2:11.

According to Genesis 37:25, Joseph's brothers sold him to a caravan of Ishmaelites, who were carrying spices, balm, and myrrh to Egypt. Then in Genesis 43:11, when there was a famine in the land of Canaan, Joseph's father told his sons to take a little honey, spices, myrrh, nuts, and almonds to Egypt to present to the governor, to buy grain, which was their brother Joseph, who they did not recognize at the time.

Myrrh mixed with wine was used in ancient culture for pleasure and relieving pain. Myrrh was used for oils, cosmetics, and the healing of diseases.

Henna

The scientific name for Henna is Lawsonia inermis. Hennas are shrubs, and some grow into small trees. Hennas are viewed by others as short hedges with dense thorny branches that protect crops, such as a vineyard from animals. The hedges also have clusters of sweet-smelling flowers that are white, yellow, or pink.

Hennas were commonly traded during biblical days and were made into a powder by drying and milling the leaves. Henna was cultivated and used in ancient times as a dyeing agent to dye hair, skin, fingernails, and fabric, and Henna is still used worldwide today.

Henna was also used as a perfume, the poetess of Song of Solomon compares her lover to a "cluster of henna blossoms from the vineyard of Engedi," Song of Solomon 1:14 NIV. Henna is only mentioned in the Song of Solomon in chapter 1:14 and 4:13; the KJV translation refers to "henna" as "camphire."

Holms or Holly Oak Tree

According to Genesis 35:8, Jacob's wife, Rebekah's nurse named Deborah, was buried under a holly oak tree outside of Bethel. Afterward, the tree was named "Allon-bacuth," which means "oak of weeping."

The holly oak is an evergreen tree known to grow over 60 feet tall but usually remains under 30 feet. The tree grows as wide as it is tall with a dense rounded crown. The holly oak leaves are glossy, bright green, and holly shaped with prickly edges. In the spring, small white flowers blossom followed by clusters of bright-red fruit in the fall.

Calabash

The calabash plant is called by several names, a gourd, bottle gourd, white-flowered gourd, long melon, but the scientific name is Lagenaria siceraria. The calabash plant can be harvested either young or at maturity.

When the calabash plant is harvested young, it can be consumed as a vegetable, when it is harvested at maturity; it is dried and made into utensils. When the calabash is young, the fruit has a light green smooth skin and white flesh. The calabash plants have a variety of shapes; they can grow to be huge and rounded, small and bottle shaped, or slim and curvy. The calabash plant can grow to be over 39 inches long.

Calabashes are used to store wine, have been made into musical instruments, like a flute, made into serving bowls, drinking containers, smoke pipes, and helmets.

The calabash produces white flowers. Gourds are mentioned 3 times in the NIV Bible, 1 Kings 6:18, 1 Kings 7:24, and 2 Kings 4:39.

According to 1 Kings 6:18 and 1 Kings 7:24, the temple paneling and round basin were decorated with carving of gourds.

According to 2 Kings 4, a young man went into the field to gather herbs and came back with wild gourds. He cooked them without realizing they were poisonous. When some of the men begin to eat the stew, after a couple of bites, they cried out, "Man of God, there is poison in this stew!" Elisha threw some flour in the pot of stew and told the men the stew was good to eat now. The men ate the stew, and they were not harmed, 2 Kings 4:39 – 41.

Broom Tree

The tree that Elijah rested under is believed by scholars to be the Retama raetam. It is also known as the broom, white broom, and the white weeping broom tree.

According to 1 King 19, Ahab told his wife, Jezebel, how Elijah had killed all the prophets of Baal. She sent a message to Elijah, saying she was going to kill him. Elijah fled for his life and traveled into the wilderness. After a day's journey, he sat down under a broom tree and prayed that he might die. Then Elijah fell asleep under the tree. The angel of the LORD touched him and told him to arise and eat; there was a baked cake on a hot stone and a jar of water for Elijah.

The broom tree shrubs are widespread in Israel's deserts, especially around Gilead, Jordan, Lebanon, and Mount Carmel. The broom tree in other Bible translations is translated as a broom shrub and juniper tree.

Myrtle

Myrtus communis is the scientific name for myrtle. Myrtle is a shrub with evergreen leaves, small white flowers blossom in the summer, and they grow on the hills about Jerusalem.

Myrtle is mentioned only in the Old Testament, a total of 6 times. The first reference of the myrtle in the Bible is in Nehemiah 8:15 regarding the celebration of the Feast of Tabernacles. The myrtle trees are mentioned 3 times in the prophet Zechariah's vision concerning "a man among the myrtle trees," Zechariah 1:8, 10, and 11.

In Hebrew, myrtle is called "hadas." In Judaism, myrtle is known as "Hadassah," and is one of the four sacred plants used by Jews during the Feast of Tabernacles, or Sukkot.

CHAPTER 22

THE CARPENTER'S SON

**"Isn't this the carpenter's son?
Isn't his mother's name Mary, and aren't his brothers
James, Joseph, Simon, and Judas?"**
Matthew 13:55 NIV

According to Matthew 13, beginning at verse 54, Jesus traveled back to his hometown with his disciples. Jesus begins to teach them in their synagogues with great power, and they were astonished.

The crowd of people begins to question each other. They asked among themselves, where did he get this power! They asked each other is this the carpenter's son and called out the names of Jesus' mother, and brothers.

Jesus' hometown crowd behavior offended him, and then Jesus said to them, "a prophet is not without honor except in his own town and in his own home," Matthew 13:57. According to Matthew 13:58, Jesus could not perform many miracles there because of their lack of faith.

Question: What is the name of Jesus' hometown? *Smile* . . .

The answer is in the back of the book

The words "Isn't this the carpenter's son" was just a typical description of Jesus by his adversaries, opposers, and his hometown. The word "carpenter" in Greek is "tekton."

Tekton can be translated into the English words "builder, workman, a craftsman in wood," and, more precisely, "carpenter."

The words "Isn't this the carpenter's son" was referring to Joseph, the husband of Mary, and the earthly father of Jesus. In the Book of Genesis, beginning in chapter 1, it can be understood that God the Father is the Sovereign Builder and the Divine Architect of the universe. Jesus is both the son of Joseph by adoption and God the Father by the divine. Jesus is the son of the "tekton" on earth and in heaven.

The people in Jesus' hometown, especially the Jewish leaders, spoke the words "Isn't this the carpenter's son" in a tone of condescension and felt contempt toward Jesus. In other words, they conveyed to Jesus, he was unworthy of respect or consideration, and the Jewish leaders had an attitude of patronizing superiority.

In Bible days, a "tekton" was an individual that performed a lowly trade or craft. His work required tiresome physical labor with his hands, and this went against both the Greek ideal of leisure and the Jewish ideal of devotion to scripture.

In ancient civilization, wood was understood as a living fabric that united heaven and earth in a "warp and weft" stitch pattern. Wood was sacred and the perfect material for building a living structure for the living man.

Note of Interests: The warp is the tightly stretched lengthwise core of fabric, while the weft is woven between the warp threads to create patterns. The weft yarn runs back and forth, and the warp runs up and down.

Wood is not like rocks, sand, or stones; it is a living plant that breathes air, and stands between heaven and earth, like a man. Wood comes from trees, which need water and nourishment to grow in stature.

When a tree is cut down, it dies. It is then cut into beams, designs, patterns, or posts that are used to build living quarters for man. Scholars believe Jesus, the carpenter's son, was familiar with plants in his life. As a growing child, Jesus probably helped Joseph with carpentry work. The kind of woods and what they crafted are not mentioned by name in the Bible. However, scholars believed they used both native and imported wood to build tables, baskets, boats, utensils, stools, houses, and other useful items.

Numerous flowering plants, fruits, and medical trees thrived in Israel. Trees that are native to Israel includes the forest of pine, tamarisk, carob, gum trees, eucalyptus, oak, olive, juniper, plane, sycamore oaks, mulberry, terebinth, cypress, sycamore-fig, pomegranate, acacia, almond, date palm, apple, cedar, poplar, willow, and the list goes on.

Note of Interests: In the study of human history through the excavation of sites, pieces of furniture were discovered constructed from willow and tamarisk wood. Coffins were found made from cypress and sycamine trees.

According to 2 Chronicles 2:16, the "cedar of Lebanon" was cut down, floated, and sent down to Joppa by sea, and then hauled to Jerusalem to construct Solomon's Temple in Jerusalem. Joppa was an ancient seaport city in Israel about 33 miles northwest of Jerusalem and approximately 65 miles from Lebanon. Lebanon is located in the Middle East, and the Mediterranean Sea borders Lebanon on the west, Israel on the south, and Syria on the east and north.

Jesus consumed plant-based food to nourish his earthly body. He used flowering spices and herbs to season his meals. Beans, citron, cucumbers, gourds, leeks, lentils, and onions are some of the vegetables and legumes Jesus would have eaten. Barley, corn, flour, millet, spelt, and wheat were the grain food in Bible days, and black cumin, cumin, dill, fennel, marjoram, oregano, and rue were some of the herbs.

According to Psalm 104:14, God provided man with herbs for the service of man.

> **He caused the grass to grow for the cattle,**
> **and herb for the service of man:**
> **that he may bring forth food out of the earth;**
> **And wine that maketh glad the heart of man,**
> **and oil to make his face to shine,**
> **and bread which strengtheneth man's heart.**
> Psalm 104:14 – 15 KJV

Jesus was familiar with edible flowering plants that produced fruits and nuts like apples, almonds, dates, figs, grapes, melons, olives, pistachios, pomegranates, and raisins.

Note of Interests: Pistachio nuts are only mentioned once in the Bible, Genesis 43:11 NIV. Jacob instructed his sons to take them as a gift to the man in control of the Egyptian food supply, which was Joseph. Melon is only mentioned once in Numbers 11, in verse 5, when the Israelites remembered what they ate in Egypt.

The 1st miracle Jesus performed was plant-related as he turned water into wine at a wedding feast his mother invited him and his disciples to in Cana in Galilee, John 2:1 – 11. Wine in biblical days was made from the juice of crushed grapes.

In the gospels of Matthew, Mark, and Luke, Jesus uses the mustard seed in two parables describing the kingdom of heaven. The mustard seed is smaller than any other seed, but it grows up to 25 feet tall, becoming as big as any other tree. The tree has pea-size flower fruits, and once ripen, it contains a single seed. The seed can be consumed raw, dried, or cooked.

Note of Interests: The mustard seed tree is also called the toothbrush tree. For hundreds of years, tender young sticks were cut from the tree and used to clean teeth.

Jesus even used flowering plants in his parables to help those who listen to understand the message. In the Gospel of Matthew 13, the tare is mentioned 8 times, and only in Matthew in a parable, Jesus spoke concerning "Wheat and Tares." Wheat and tares look identical in the beginning stages of its growth, but while wheat produces seeds, the tare is more like a flower. The tare is considered a weed, which grows among the wheat. The "tare" that Jesus described in His parable was also known as the "darnel seed," which is also called "false wheat."

In Luke 12:22 – 34, some Bible scholars and botanists believe that the Chamomile was the plant Jesus was referring to in this parable. Jesus rebuked the disciples for being concerned about clothing and promised that God would take care of them just as He clothes the grass of the field. Chamomile is native to Israel and blooms with tiny daisy-like flowers.

Note of Interests: Chamomile or camomile is the common name for several daisy-like plants of the family Asteraceae.

~

Other essential plants in Jesus' era were cotton and flax, which were woven into fabric and made into garments. The papyrus plants were used for making writing paper, and reeds were made into baskets, boats, and cradles.

The olive trees provided oil for lighting lamps and used in cooking. In Matthew 25, Jesus gave a parable of the 10 virgins. Five of the 10 virgins took their lamps and took oil in jars along with their lamps, and the 5 foolish virgins did not.

The olive oil is one of the ingredients in the anointing oil mixture, along with myrrh, sweet cinnamon, sweet calamus, cassia, Exodus 30:23 – 26 KJV. The oil was used to sanctify the priests, the tabernacle, and the tabernacle articles. Olive oil was used as part of the grain offering, along with choice flour and sprinkle with frankincense. Kings and individuals were anointed with olive oil as a sign that they were chosen by God to rule.

Note of Interests: According to Genesis 28, Jacob anointed a stone as a memorial to God, and named the place "Bethel," which means "house of God." Remember, Jacob had a dream there, where he saw a stairway that reached from earth to heaven, and the angels of God were going up and down the stairway? Genesis 28:10 – 22. The anointing oil was used for the sacred purpose of "sanctifying or setting apart" a person, place, or article for God's exclusive use.

<hr>

PS: If you do not remember the biblical event concerning Jacob's dream at Bethel in Genesis 28, take a moment, and be blessed . . . read it three times, straight. Hallelujah is the Highest Praise.

CHAPTER 23
FLOWERING PLANTS LISTING

A list of the flowering plants discussed in this book is recorded in this chapter. Some of the flowering plants are mentioned in more than one chapter, but it is only listed once. In chapter 1, there is no flowering plant discussed. However, fig tree, lilies, and myrrh are mentioned in Bible verses that were used to explain man's life, but not discussed in a brief or long sentence(s) or paragraph(s).

A short line has been provided by each flowering plant, so you can check it off once you view that plant. The scientific and common names are given, for most, and the scientific name will take you directly to a picture of the flowering plant. I pray you take time, in your quiet time with the LORD, to look at a picture of the listed plants, the LORD's creation. It does not have to be done all in one day; it could be one a day or once a week. Be Blessed in Jesus' Name. Amen.

Don't forget, a plant can have several "common names," depending on the region, but only one "scientific name." The scientific name always consists of two-names; the first name identifies the plant's Genus, the group of species to which it belongs, and the genus name is capitalized; the second name is an adjective that describes the individual species, and that name is in lowercase. For example, Punica granatum; there are more than one Punica, but only one Punica granatum.

There are approximately 13,000 known genera and around 290,000 known species in the diverse flowering plant group. There can be hundreds of plants named in the same genera. Therefore, the species in the genera that Bible scholars believe are referred to in the Bible are listed, or the most popular species in Israel.

Chapter 2 Pomegranate

Pomegranate Trees:

____	Punica granatum is the scientific name for the pomegranate tree.

____	Punica protopunica is the scientific name for a smaller pomegranate tree.

Chapter 3	Inverted Flowers

Fig Trees:

____	Ficus carica is the scientific name for the common fig tree.

____	Ficus sycomorus is the scientific name for the sycamore-fig tree.

Chapter 4	Thorns and Thistles

Thistles:

____	Notobasis syriaca is the scientific name for the Syrian thistle. It is believed to be the "thorns" that suffocated the grain in Jesus' parable, and what Gideon's whip was made from.

___ Scolymus maculatus is the scientific name for the spotted golden thistle.

___ Cynara cardunculus is the scientific name for the artichoke thistle.

___ Silybum marianum is the scientific name for the holy milk thistle.

___ Echinops ritro is the scientific name for the cherry purple globe thistle.

___ Silybum marianum is the scientific name for the milk thistle.

___ Sarcopoterium spinosum is the scientific name for the thorny burnett thistle believed to be the thistle used for making the "crown of thorns" that was placed on Jesus' head.

___ Ziziphus Spina-christ is the scientific name for the Christ's thorn jujube, another thistle some scholars believe was the "crown of thorns."

___ Paliurus spina-christi is the scientific name for the Jerusalem thorn, another low thorny plant believed to be used by the Roman soldiers in making a "crown of thorns" for Jesus' head.

Tumbleweed and Poppies are often considered thistles but are not.

___ Papaver somniferum is the scientific name for the poppy plant.

Tumbleweeds:

____ Salsola tragus
____ Salsola iberica
____ Salsola kali
____ Salsola australis
____ Salsola pestifer

Chapter 5   Olive and Olives

____ Olea europaea is the scientific name for the olive tree.
____ Cinnamomum verum is the scientific name for the cinnamon plant.
____ Acorus calamus is the scientific name for the calamus plant.
____ Cinnamomum cassia is the scientific name for the cassia plant.

Chapter 6   Mandrakes

____ Mandragora autumnalis is the scientific name for the mandrake plant.

Chapter 7   Sold His Birthright

Pulse Crops believed to be eaten by Daniel and his friends while in Babylonian.

____ Len culinaris is the scientific name for lentils.
____ Vicia fabal is the scientific name for broad beans.
____ Vicia fabal is the scientific name for chickpea.

Chapter 8   The Rose of Sharon

Rose of Sharon's Debate:

____   Hibiscus syriarus is the scientific name for the "rose of Sharon."

____   Sharon Tulip, scholars claim the rose of Sharon was a red tulip. Other scholars believe that the "rose of Sharon" may have been one of these flowering plants.

____   Crocus

____   Madonna Lily

____   Narcissus Rose

____   Wild Hyacinth

____   Crown Daisy

Chapter 9   Lilies

____   Lilium candidum is the scientific name for the true lily, known as the Madonna lily.

____   Lilium longiforum is the scientific name for the Easter lily; this lily has become the traditional flower of Easter, symbolizes "the resurrection" of Jesus.

____   Nyphaea caerulea is the scientific name for the Lotus of the Nile. It is believed that the Lotus of Nile is the one mentioned in 1 Kings 7:26 and 2 Chronicles 4:5.

Chapter 10   A Tenth

Mints, Dill, and Cumin:

____   Mentha longifolia is the scientific name for horsemint; believed to be the mint Jesus is referring to in His discourse with the Pharisees.

____ Mentha spicata is the scientific name for spearmint.

____ Anethum graveolens is the scientific name for dill, (anise in KJV).

____ Cuminum cyminum is the scientific name for cumin.

____ Coriandrum sativum is the scientific name for coriander.

Chapter 11   Toxic Oleander

____ Nerium oleander is the scientific name for the oleander plant. Scholars believe the Nerium oleander was used to sweeten the bitter waters, and the tree planted by the streams of water, which bring forth his fruit in due seasons.

____ The "Rose of Jericho" is thought to refer to the oleander by some scholars. However, in traditional beliefs, the "Rose of Jericho" is a "tumbleweed" that followed Jesus while he was in the desert for 40 days and nights. The most popular oleanders are listed below.

____ Algiers

____ Calypso

____ Hardy Red

____ Petite Salmon

____ Sister Agnes

Chapter 12   The Gifts

____ Commiphora myrrha is the scientific name for myrrh.

____ Boswellia sacra is the scientific name for frankincense.

Chapter 13   Hyssop

____   Origanum syriacum is the scientific name for hyssop.

Chapter 14   Barley and Wheat

____   Hordeum vulgare is the scientific name for barley.

____   Secale cerale is the scientific name for rye.

____   Avena sativa is the scientific name for oat.

____   Vitis vinifera is the scientific name for the common grape.

____   Zea mays is the scientific name for maize, also known as corn.

____   Triticum aestivum is the scientific name for the common wheat, also known as bread wheat.

____   Triticum compositum is the scientific name for the Egyptian wheat. Scholars believe this is the type of wheat Pharaoh saw in his dream, Genesis 41.

____   Triticum vulgare is the scientific name for the wheat that will sometimes produce one hundred grains in the ear. Scholars believe this is the wheat Jesus was referring to in his parable about wheat sowed on good ground, Matthew 13.

____   Triticum spelta is the scientific name for spelt, an inferior wheat.

Chapter 15   Flax to Linen

____   Linum usitatissimum is the scientific name for flax.

Chapter 16   Bulrushes

The word "bulrush" is a common name for large wetland, grassy-like plants in the sedge plant family called Cyperaceae.

____   Cyperus papyrus is the scientific name for papyrus, which is believed to be the "ark of bulrushes" baby Moses was placed in by his mother.

____   Schoenoplectus acutus is the scientific name for a bulrush that grows between 3 to 10 feet tall.

____   Bolboschoenus maritimus is the scientific name for bulrush grows about 4 feet in height.

Chapter 17   Altar of Incense

____   Styrax officinalis is the scientific name for the stacte plant.

____   Styrax tonkinensis is the scientific name for the onycha plant.

____   Astragaius tragacantha is the scientific name for the tragacanth plant.

____   Ferula gummosa is the scientific name for galbanum plant.

Chapter 18   The Prodigal Son

____   Ceratonia siliquar is the scientific name for the carob tree.

Chapter 19   Seven Fresh Bowstrings

____   Thymelaea hirsute is the scientific name for yitran, also called mitran.

Chapter 20   Castor Oil Plant

____   Ricinus communis is the scientific name for the castor oil shrub.

Chapter 21   Biblical Events Surrounding Plants

____   Cercis siliquastrum is the scientific name for the Judas' tree.

____   Tamarix syriaca is the scientific name for the tamarisk tree.

____   Vitex agnus-castus is the scientific name for Abraham's bush.

____   Euonymus alatus is the scientific name for Moses' burning bush.

____   Aloe vera is the scientific name for the aloe plant.

____   Lawsonia inermis is the scientific name for the menna plant.

____   Quercus ilex is the scientific name for the holms/holly oak tree.

____   Lagenaria siceraria is the scientific name for the calabash tree.

____   Retama raetam is the scientific name for the broom tree.

____   Myrtus communis is the scientific name for the myrtle tree.

Chapter 22   The Carpenter's Son

____   Pinus pinea is the scientific name for the pine tree.

____   Pinus halepensis is the scientific name for the Aleppo
pine in Jerusalem.

____   Eucalyptus regnans is the scientific name for the
eucalyptus tree.

____   Juniperus oxycedrus is the scientific name for the
juniper tree.

____   Acer pseudoplatanus is the scientific name for the
plane tree.

____   Pistacia terebinthus is the scientific name for the
terebinth tree.

____   Pistacia vera is the scientific name for the pistachio
tree.

____   Cupressus sempervirens is the scientific name for the
cypress tree.

____   Acacia tortilis is the scientific name for the acacia
tree.

____   Populus alba is the scientific name for the white
poplar tree.

____   Salix salicina is the scientific name for the willow
tree.

____   Cedrus libani is the scientific name for the cedar of
Lebanon's trees.

____   Citrus medica is the scientific name for the citron
plant.

____   Cucumis sativus is the scientific name for the
cucumber plant.

____   Cucumis melo is the scientific name for melons.

____   Allium porrum is the scientific name for the leek
plant.

____ Urginea maritima is the scientific name for the onion plant.

____ Pennisetum glaucum is the scientific name for the millet plant.

____ Nigelia sativa is the scientific name for the black cumin plant.

____ Foeniculum vulgare is the scientific name for the fennel plant.

____ Origanum majorana is the scientific name for the marjoram plant.

____ Origanum vulgare is the scientific name for the oregano plant.

____ Ruta graveolens is the scientific name for the rue plant.

____ Calotropis procera is the scientific name for the apple of Sodom.

____ Prunus dulcis is the scientific name for the almond tree.

____ Phoenix dactylifera is the scientific name for the date or date palm tree.

____ Brassica juncea is the scientific name for the mustard seed plant.

____ Chamaemelum nobile is the scientific name for the daisy-like plant Chamomile.

A READER'S QUESTION

This new section just dropped in my spirit at 0613 on January 14, 2017, titled A Reader's Question.

Question: In so many words, he asked, "Isn't it hard to come home from working a regular job, and work on the book, almost every day?"

Answer: I don't believe I have to work on the book every day, but I enjoy it. I'm pleased with this assignment I feel "Father God" has given me.

When I feel weary or tired, I ask Him for strength. When my thoughts are few, I ask Him to anoint my mind, intellect, and thinking process. I ask Father God to bring knowledge, education, past teaching, and learning to my remembrance, and His revelation to my heart and spirit by His Holy Spirit. All I need is just one touch by the Master . . . Sah-sha-ba-tha-tha-dob-oshee . . . Just one touch, Hallelujah!

I give him praise every morning when I rise, and I worship Him while I have a light breakfast, I pray to Him throughout the day. I also fast a day, or two, almost every week, and sometimes longer.

The days that I have had health issues, I remind Father God in a politely loving humble prayer that I am human, and if He doesn't give me strength, the mindset, or the burning desire, I can't do His work. I end my prayer something like this, "I assume, You want me to rest, today, this evening, or for two or three days. In Jesus' Name. Amen."

Note of Interests: I just felt the unction of the Holy Spirit, Hallelujah! In Matthew 26, when Jesus was in the Garden of Gethsemane, praying with his disciples, they fell asleep. When Jesus found them sleeping, He woke them up and told them, "the spirit is willing, but the flesh is weak," Matthew 26:41. Jesus was not mad or upset with them, nor did He cast them away; He was strongly encouraging them to beware of the weakness of the flesh. I believe fasting always strengthen the flesh!

PS: Note of Interests' revelation was just placed in my spirit, Saturday, July 25, 2020, around 10:53 am, give or take a few minutes. Praise God!

**In all thy ways acknowledge him,
and he shall direct thy paths.**
Proverbs 3:6 KJV

AUTHOR'S CLOSING REMARKS

I Love This, Praise God! I pray you do, too.

I enjoyed writing this book; it was interesting, exciting, and amazing to me. I will forever view flowering plants in a different light. I was educated about God's beautiful creations.

One thing I have learned is that plants will grow, and the flowers will bloom, fade, wilt, and die. There are plants that need to be sown every year, others only once. Some plant blossoms are displayed only part of the year, and others all-year-around. Most plants blossom in spring and others in summer, winter, and fall. When a plant blossoms, it means it is at its most dazzling, gleaming, phenomenal earthy life moments.

Pray for the Ministry . . .

May the "Prince of Peace," Bless You, Blossoms Your Life, and Give You His Perfect Peace."

Dr. Vanessa

REFERENCES

Chapter 1
1. BibleGateway: https://www.biblegateway.com
2. Wikipedia, The Free Encyclopedia: https://en.wikipedia.org/wiki/Flower

Chapter 2
1. BibleGateway: https://www.biblegateway.com
2. Wikipedia, The Free Encyclopedia: https://en.wikipedia.org/wiki/Pomegranate

Chapter 3
1. BibleGateway: https://www.biblegateway.com
2. Wikipedia, The Free Encyclopedia: https://en.wikipedia.org/wiki/Common_fig
3. Wikipedia, The Free Encyclopedia: https://en.wikipedia.org/wiki/Gilgal_I

Chapter 4
1. BibleGateway: https://www.biblegateway.com
2. Wikipedia, The Free Encyclopedia: https://en.wikipedia.org/wiki/Thistle

Chapter 5
1. BibleGateway: https://www.biblegateway.com
2. Wikipedia, The Free Encyclopedia: https://en.wikipedia.org/wiki/Mount_of_Olives

Chapter 6
1. BibleGateway: https://www.biblegateway.com
2. Wikipedia, The Free Encyclopedia: https://en.wikipedia.org/wiki/Herbaceous_plants
3. Wikipedia, The Free Encyclopedia: https://en.wikipedia.org/wiki/Mandragora_autumnalis

Chapter 7
1. BibleGateway: https://www.biblegateway.com
2. Wikipedia, The Free Encyclopedia: https://en.wikipedia.org/wiki/Jacob_and_Esau

Chapter 8
1. BibleGateway: https://www.biblegateway.com
2. Wikipedia, The Free Encyclopedia: https://en.wikipedia.org/wiki/Rose_of_Sharon

Chapter 9
1. BibleGateway: https://www.biblegateway.com
2. Wikipedia, The Free Encyclopedia: https://en.wikipedia.org/wiki/Lilium

Chapter 10
1. BibleGateway: https://www.biblegateway.com
2. Wikipedia, The Free Encyclopedia: https://en.wikipedia.org/wiki/Herb
3. Wikipedia, The Free Encyclopedia: https://en.wikipedia.org/wiki/Spices

Chapter 11
1. Wikipedia, The Free Encyclopedia: https://en.wikipedia.org/wiki/Nerium

Chapter 12
1. BibleGateway: https://www.biblegateway.com
2. Wikipedia, The Free Encyclopedia: https://en.wikipedia.org/wiki/Myrrh
3. Wikipedia, The Free Encyclopedia: https://en.wikipedia.org/wiki/Frankincense

Chapter 13
1. BibleGateway: https://www.biblegateway.com
2. Wikipedia, The Free Encyclopedia: https://en.wikipedia.org/wiki/Origanum_syriacum

Chapter 14
1. BibleGateway: https://www.biblegateway.com
2. Wikipedia, The Free Encyclopedia: https://en.wikipedia.org/wiki/Barley
3. Wikipedia, The Free Encyclopedia: https://en.wikipedia.org/wiki/Wheat

Chapter 15
1. BibleGateway: https://www.biblegateway.com
2. Wikipedia, The Free Encyclopedia: https://en.wikipedia.org/wiki/Flax
3. Wikipedia, The Free Encyclopedia: https://en.wikipedia.org/wiki/Linen

Chapter 16
1. BibleGateway: https://www.biblegateway.com
2. Wikipedia, The Free Encyclopedia: https://en.wikipedia.org/wiki/Cyperus_papyrus
3. Wikipedia, The Free Encyclopedia: https://en.wikipedia.org/wiki/Bulrush

Chapter 17
1. BibleGateway: https://www.biblegateway.com
2. Wikipedia, The Free Encyclopedia: https://en.wikipedia.org/wiki/Stacte
3. Wikipedia, The Free Encyclopedia: https://en.wikipedia.org/wiki/Onycha
4. Wikipedia, The Free Encyclopedia: https://en.wikipedia.org/wiki/Galbanum

Chapter 18
1. BibleGateway: https://www.biblegateway.com
2. Wikipedia, The Free Encyclopedia: https://en.wikipedia.org/wiki/Carob

Chapter 19
1. BibleGateway: https://www.biblegateway.com
2. Jacksonville Theological Seminary: Philistines
3. Wikipedia, The Free Encyclopedia: https://en.wikipedia.org/wiki/Thymelaea_hirsuta

Chapter 20
1. BibleGateway: https://www.biblegateway.com
2. Wikipedia, The Free Encyclopedia: https://en.wikipedia.org/wiki/Ricinus

Chapter 21
1. BibleGateway: https://www.biblegateway.com
2. Wikipedia, The Free Encyclopedia: https://en.wikipedia.org/wiki/Cercis_siliquastrum
3. Wikipedia, The Free Encyclopedia: https://en.wikipedia.org/wiki/Tamarix
4. Wikipedia, The Free Encyclopedia: https://en.wikipedia.org/wiki/Vitex_agnus-castus

5. Wikipedia, The Free Encyclopedia: https://en.wikipedia.org/wiki/Euonymus_alatus
6. Wikipedia, The Free Encyclopedia: https://en.wikipedia.org/wiki/Aloe_vera
7. Wikipedia, The Free Encyclopedia: https://en.wikipedia.org/wiki/Commiphora_myrrha
8. Wikipedia, The Free Encyclopedia: https://en.wikipedia.org/wiki/Lawsonia_inermis
9. Wikipedia, The Free Encyclopedia: https://en.wikipedia.org/wiki/Holly
10. Wikipedia, The Free Encyclopedia: https://en.wikipedia.org/wiki/Calabash
11. Wikipedia, The Free Encyclopedia: https://en.wikipedia.org/wiki/Retama
12. Wikipedia, The Free Encyclopedia: https://en.wikipedia.org/wiki/Myrtus_communis

Chapter 22

1. BibleGateway: https://www.biblegateway.com
2. Wikipedia, The Free Encyclopedia: https://en.wikipedia.org/wiki/Tekton
3. Wikipedia, The Free Encyclopedia: https://en.wikipedia.org/wiki/Chamomile

ANSWERS & INFORMATION SECTION

Chapter 2
1. Pison
2. Gihon
3. Hiddekel
4. Euphrates

The first group of High Priests was Aaron, Nadab, Abihu, Eleazar, and Ithamar. Exodus 28:1, Exodus 39:26 – 27.

The name of the two pillars was Jachin on the right, and Boaz on the left, 1 Kings 7:21.

Chapter 5
1. Spain
2. Italy
3. Malta
4. Greece
5. Turkey
6. Syria
7. Cyprus
8. Lebanon
9. Israel
10. Palestine
11. Egypt
12. Libya

The two mountains, in which the Israelites are to read the blessing and cursing of the LORD are Mount Gerizim and Mount Ebal, Deuteronomy 27:11 – 13.

Moses told the people after they have crossed the Jordan River, the tribes of Simeon, Levi, Judah, Issachar, Joseph, and Benjamin would stand on Mount Gerizim and read the blessings to the people. The tribes of Reuben, Gad, Asher, Zebulun, Dan, and Naphtali would stand on Mount Ebal, and read the curses from the LORD.

Chapter 11
The place where the bitter waters were found, what was it later named? Marah

When they (Israel) came to Marah, they could not drink its water because it was bitter; that is why the place is called Marah, Exodus 15:23 NIV.

Chapter 15
Joseph of Arimathea and Nicodemus a Pharisee and member of the Sanhedrin, John 19:38 – 40.

Chapter 19
The other two Nazarites for life are Samuel, and John the Baptist, 1 Samuel 1:11 and Luke 1:15.

Chapter 22
Jesus' birthplace is the city of Bethlehem, which is in Judea, near Jerusalem.

Jesus grew up in a little town called Nazareth of Galilee. Jesus moved to Capernaum from his hometown at the beginning of his ministry.